Orange County Fare

Orange County *Fare*

A Culinary Journey Through the California Riviera

Published by
The Junior League of Orange County, California, Inc.
Copyright © 2009 by
The Junior League of Orange County, California, Inc.
5140 Campus Drive
Newport Beach, California 92660
949-261-1837

This cookbook is a collection of our favorite recipes,
which are not necessarily original recipes.

Library of Congress Control Number: 2009924982
ISBN: 978-0-9818458-0-7

Edited, Designed and Produced by

Favorite Recipes® Press

An imprint of

FRP.INC

A wholly owned subsidiary of
Southwestern/Great American, Inc.
P.O. Box 305142
Nashville, Tennessee 37230
800-358-0560

Art Director and Book Design: Steve Newman
Project Editor: Tanis Westbrook

Manufactured in the United States of America
First Printing 2009
10,000 copies

**JUNIOR LEAGUE OF
ORANGE COUNTY, CALIFORNIA, INC.**
Women building better communities

Mixed Sources
Product group from well-managed
forests, controlled sources and
recycled wood or fiber
www.fsc.org Cert no. SW-COC-003334
© 1996 Forest Stewardship Council

FSC

Orange County *Fare*

a culinary journey through the California Riviera

Presented by
The Junior League of Orange County,
California, Inc.

COOKBOOK COMMITTEE

Orange County Fare: A Culinary Journey Through the California Riviera has been in production for nearly two years, led by a talented and dedicated committee of women who have worked tirelessly expending many, many hours on this project. The Cookbook Committee would like to thank the members of the Junior League, whose commitment to excellence has made this book possible. We also give our heartfelt appreciation to our friends and families for their endless sacrifices, constant support and encouragement, patience, and good humor during the production of this book. We could not have done it without you.

Steering Committee

Chair
Kathy Kelly

Recipe Chair
Kate Rader

Sales Chair
Michelle Stiegler

Treasurer
Dana McCollum

Chair-Elect
Karen Kroeter

Design and Editing Chair
Tristan Ritter

Business Support Chair
Noelle Gamber

Sustainer Advisor
Susie Luer

Marketing and PR Chair
Sherryl Brightwell

Assistant-at-Large
Courtney Blackwell

Recipe Testing

Megan Brief
Kim Bucher
Carrie Campbell
Oma Talley Cast

Kim Domer
Heidi Endert
Amy Grady
Molly Jolly

Melissa McGee
Stacy Nichols
Yuki Pitkin
Lisa Rhoads

Julie Robbins
Shanna Siegel
Tanya von Mittenwald
Lori Wagner

Design and Editing

Carla Craft
Nicole Hager
Shannon Spencer
Bita Karabian

Copywriting

Courtney Blackwell
Kathy Kelly
Karen Kroeter

Marketing and PR

Patricia Beaulieu
Christine Michaud
Claudia Rich
Amy Yovan

Sales

Carissa Rains Beyer
Carrie Campbell
Deanna Garcia
Jennifer Henderson
Amy Reardon

Board of Directors

2007–2008 JLOCC Board of Directors

President
Stacey Kinney

Vice President
Sarah Dressler

Secretary
Jennifer Martin

Treasurer/Finance Director
Carla Dillon

President-Elect
Erin Stone

Communications Director
Kathryn Grant

Community Director
Gwen Black

Fund Development Director
Liana Augustini

Membership Director
Laura Giles

Projects Director
Isabelle Ord

Training Director
MeeRan Kim Anderson

Sustainer Adviser
Janet Colclaser

Board Assistant
Kristin Scheithauer

2008–2009 JLOCC Board of Directors

President
Erin Stone

Vice President
Nedka Stills

Secretary
Carla Poulin

Treasurer/Finance Director
Laurel Murray

President-Elect
Kathryn Grant

Communications Director
Poppy Holguin

Community Director
Meredith Cagle

Fund Development Director
Mara Hampton

Membership Director
April Young

Projects Director
Kelly Cornell

Training Director
Denise Scott

Sustainer Adviser
Anne Nutt

Board Assistant
Megan Lester

Orange County Fare Sponsors

Sous Chef

Maralou Harrington

The Jacqueline M. Glass and Richard and Joanna James Families

Jaynine & Dave Warner

Culinarian

Earth Friendly Products

Photo Sponsorships

Stacey Kinney

Kim & Ferari Vu

Gracey & Al Weisbrod

Gold Plate

Sherryl L. Brightwell

Susan & David Crockett

Diva Domestica

Phyllis R. Drayton

Kathy & Charles Kelly

Karen & Ben Kroeter

Susie & Mark Luer

Erin & John Stone

Orange County Fare Sponsors

Silver Plate

Victoria Firestone Ackerman

Gwendolyn Black

Sophie Hall Cripe

Laura Giles

Kathryn Grant

JLOCC Sustainers

Dawn & Steve Leavitt

Charlene Lee

Hilary & Jay Meurer

Margaret Ogden Morgan

Anne B. Nutt

Carla A. Poulin

Michelle & Jason Stiegler

Dr. Sandra P. Thompson

Catherine A. Treinen

Tanya von Mittenwald

Janine Wald

Shannon & Gene Zech

Bronze Plate

2008–2009 Finance Council

Betty Adkinson

MeeRan Anderson

Viki L. Barie

Barbara C. Barned

Courtney Blackwell

Cathie Cardelucci

Caring Companions at Home

Terri Carr

Susan S. Champion

The Cohen Family

Kathy & Paul Cornell

Kelly E. Cornell

Dr. & Mrs. Richard E. Cramm

Carla & Peter Dillon

Janet W. Eggers

Francine Eskenzai

Maura Ferrero-Baroni

Christy Flanagan

Camille Foster

Cindy Fung

Susanne Guy

Mara & George Hampton

Lori A. Hawkins

Poppy Holguin

Mary-Kathryn Jarcy

Ms. Karen O. Johnson

Olivia Johnson

Melissa Leasure

Jennifer J. Martin

Melinda B. McCrea

Carolyn McInerney

Heather McKenzie

Christine B. Moore

Anastasia Orbacz

Leslie Ordonez

The Rader Family

Tristan H. Ritter

The Rowe Family

Linda Ruben

Denise Scott

Nedka Stills

Lauren Stock

Mrs. Sandra Teitsworth

Leta Warmington

Karen Beilsmith Warren

Grace & Ronald Wright

Special Acknowledgments

*O*n behalf of The Junior League of Orange County, California, Inc., we would like to extend a special thank-you to our photographer, Marc Weisberg, for donating his talent and time to our book. Your beautiful photographs and creative vision have made this book a treasure for generations to enjoy.

Thank you for your support and generosity to the Junior League of Orange County, California, Inc.

The Ritz-Carlton, Laguna Niguel

Thank you for providing the gorgeous location for our cover photo.

Mr. & Mrs. Fritz L. Duda

Kathryn & Robert Grant

Karla & Tom Hammond

Thank you for allowing us to photograph your beautiful homes and boats for our book.

Letia Short

Susan Ballou, Ballou Communications

Thank you for your invaluable support and advice.

FOREWORD

We live in Paradise! The "California Riviera" is made up of beautiful landscapes, sprawling beaches, glorious sunsets, and the most philanthropic people I have ever met. We are so fortunate to live in a place where the community comes together—to support a good cause, a great chef, a new dining venture.

Just off the sand, or on the coast, and inland far and wide, you will find great cooks, grand chefs, and local restaurants that share delicious dishes.

I have had the tasty pleasure of getting to know many of the food lovers in The OC, and their dishes make up the heart of where we live. They come from all walks of life, varied places, and diverse cultures. And when we all come together, we share our signature dishes and a passion to give back to this fine place we call home.

This collection of recipes will take you, the cook, on a tour of Orange County through recipes, photographs, and stories. Almost five hundred recipes were submitted by Junior League members, families, friends, neighborhood restaurants, and local chefs, and the recipes have ultimately made their way into this collection to represent, support, and sustain our communities. The Junior League of Orange County, California, Inc., commits indefinite time and energy to numerous local charities, organizations, and projects, and the proceeds from this book will benefit all of them.

In addition to revealing culinary secrets, this wealth of recipes shares hearts and minds and traditions, bringing us closer together and allowing us to make a difference where we live. I am proud to support The Junior League of Orange County, California, Inc., and when you read this foreword you should be, too. You made a difference today, and in turn, gained the one thing that I believe brings us all closer together...Fabulous Food!

I am so grateful to live in Orange County and so proud to support an organization of women committed to promoting voluntarism and improving the community. On behalf of The Junior League of Orange County, California, Inc., thank you for your support and for taking a "Culinary Journey Through the California Riviera."

Eat Well,

Jamie Gwen

Jamie Gwen
Radio & T.V. Host
www.chefjamie.com

CONTENTS

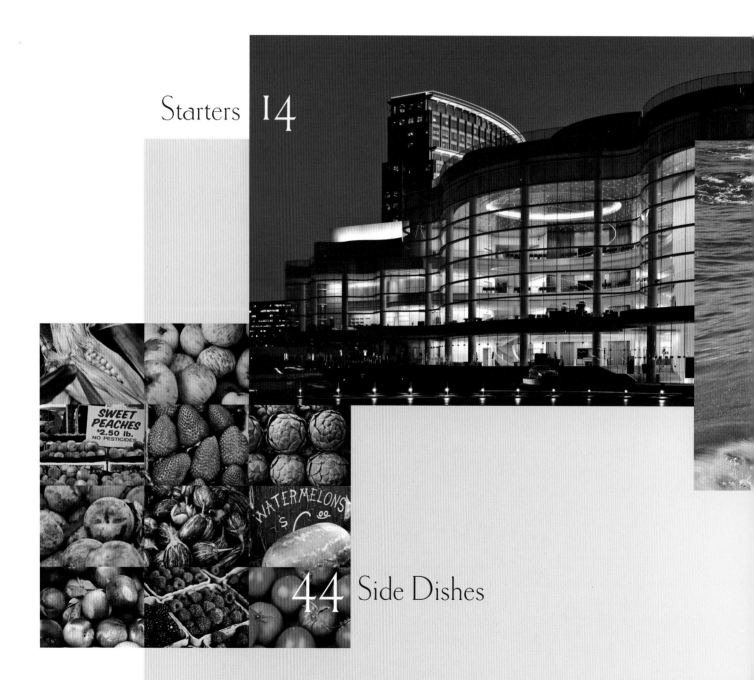

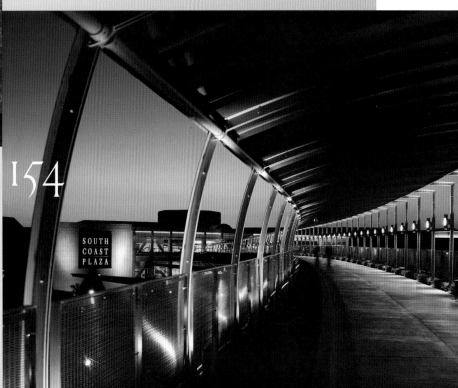

INTRODUCTION

*W*elcome to *Orange County Fare: A Culinary Journey Through the California Riviera.* We hope you enjoy this special collection of our favorite recipes and the photographic tour of "The OC." Pop culture has created quite a reputation for Orange County. From housewives to high-schoolers, "The OC" is perceived as a place of utter extravagance. So, you might wonder about a cookbook from the county where the extent of culinary savvy is making reservations, or so you'd think.

Unquestionably, we are privileged to live in such a wonderful and diverse place. Sure, the sunshine and sandy beaches do influence the Orange County culture. But our community is truly shaped by the composite of diverse culture, range of city life, and local history found here.

Since its founding as the Newport Harbor Service League in 1956, The Junior League of Orange County, California, Inc., has had an extraordinary impact on the Orange County community. It was the Junior League that initiated the Volunteer Center of Orange County, New Directions for Women, and Court Appointed Special Advocates of Orange County, Inc. In 1981, the Junior League made the first public donation to enable the establishment of Orangewood Children's Home.

Over the years, the Junior League has collaborated with Boys and Girls Clubs of Garden Grove and San Juan Capistrano, Girls Inc., Orange County Children's Therapeutic Arts Center, Human Options, Orange County Bar Foundation, YMCA of Orange County, Casa Teresa, Olive Crest, Laura's House, and Orangewood Children's Foundation. These are only some examples of The Junior League of Orange County, California, Inc.'s legacy of community collaboration and impact.

The Junior League continues to seek out and provide support for underserved needs in our community. The Junior League is partnering once again with Orangewood Children's Foundation to provide programming for The Orangewood Children's Foundation Academy, a residential high school for dependent youth in Orange County, to give students a stable high school experience and equip them for success after graduation.

It is through support of our donors, the strength of our collaborations, and the talent and commitment of our members that the Junior League makes its impact. Junior League volunteers give thousands of hours in service each year and since the organization's founding have raised more than $7 million.

Through opportunities for training and development, the Junior League invests in its members, providing development and training so that members can cultivate new skills in a supportive environment and apply them to their job, their family, and out into the community to make an even greater impact. Junior League women have gone on to serve on community boards, earn high-level positions with nonprofit organizations, grow into new careers and industries, and hold public office. Truly, the Junior League is a collaboration of Women Building Better Communities®.

In the present, we strive to carry our legacy forward, looking always to the future. We hope *Orange County Fare* will inspire many joyful meals and that the work of the Junior League will inspire enthusiasm for voluntarism and service. Thank you for being part of our legacy.

MISSION STATEMENT

The Junior League of Orange County, California, Inc., is an organization of women committed to promoting voluntarism, developing the potential of women, and improving the community through the effective action and leadership of trained volunteers.

Its purpose is exclusively educational and charitable. The Junior League of Orange County, California, Inc., reaches out to women of all races, religions, or national origins who demonstrate an interest in and commitment to voluntarism.

Curtains Up

STARTERS

*O*range County boasts a vivacious arts and cultural scene. With state-of-the-art performance venues, cultural museums, historical points of interest, thriving artist districts, and world-renowned festivals, Orange County has become the arts capital of Southern California.

The Orange County Performing Arts Center is the jewel of Costa Mesa. With the addition of the beautiful Renee and Henry Segerstrom Concert Hall and the Samueli Theater in 2006, OCPAC continues to be a world-class destination for the best the performing arts has to offer. It is also home to the Pacific Symphony, the Philharmonic Society of Orange County, and the Pacific Chorale.

The city of Laguna Beach is home to not only some of Southern California's most beautiful vistas, but is also the hub of visual arts. A well-known artist colony, Laguna Beach is the place to gallery hop. The first Thursday of each month, galleries open their doors for the Laguna Art Walk. Each summer, Laguna Beach hosts the Laguna Arts Festival featuring its most famous attraction, The Pageant of the Masters, a show of "living pictures" where real people pose to look like their counterparts in famous works of art.

Orange County arts draw on a creative and culturally diverse population of artists, both visual and performing, to make it one of the most inspiring places to be.

Chicken Mango Lettuce Bundles with Ginger Dipping Sauce

Serves 6 to 10

Ginger Dipping Sauce

3 tablespoons rice wine vinegar

2 tablespoons light soy sauce

2 tablespoons water

1 tablespoon finely chopped
    fresh gingerroot

2 teaspoons chili pepper

Chicken Filling and Assembly

4 cups shredded cooked chicken

6 scallions, thinly sliced

6 to 10 fresh basil leaves, chopped

6 to 10 fresh mint leaves, chopped

1 tablespoon grapeseed oil

Juice of 1 or 2 limes

1 head butter lettuce

1 mango, cut into thin strips

1 red bell pepper, cut into strips

1 cup bean sprouts

Dipping Sauce

Combine the vinegar, soy sauce, water, gingerroot and chili pepper in a small bowl and mix well.

Filling and Assembly

Combine the chicken with the scallions, basil, mint, grapeseed oil and lime juice in a large bowl and mix well.

Separate the lettuce into large leaves for the wrappers. Arrange the lettuce on a platter. Arrange the filling, dipping sauce, mango, bell pepper and bean sprouts on the platter. Allow guests to prepare bundles to their individual tastes.

Bacon-Wrapped Dates with Goat Cheese

Makes 24

24 dates
3 ounces goat cheese
12 slices bacon

Soak twenty-four wooden picks in water in a bowl for 10 minutes; drain. Cut the dates open, leaving one side intact. Spoon the goat cheese into the dates and press the sides to enclose the filling. Cut the bacon slices crosswise into halves. Wrap each date with a slice of bacon and secure with a wooden pick.

Preheat the oven to 375 degrees. Arrange the dates on a baking sheet and bake for 20 minutes. Turn the dates over and bake for 10 to 20 minutes longer or until the bacon is crisp; drain on paper towels.

Aussie Sausage Rolls and Dip

Serves 10 to 12

Honey Dijon Dip
1 cup mayonnaise
2 tablespoons Dijon mustard
2 tablespoons honey

Aussie Sausage Rolls
1 (16-ounce) package frozen puff
    pastry, thawed
1¹/₂ pounds sage-flavor sausage links
    or other sausage links
Paprika to taste

Dip
Combine the mayonnaise, Dijon mustard and honey in a bowl and mix well. Chill in the refrigerator.

Sausage Rolls
Preheat the oven to 350 degrees. Roll the pastry ¹/₈ inch thick on a lightly floured surface. Arrange a row of sausage links end to end along the narrow edge of the pastry. Roll the pastry to enclose the links, cutting away excess pastry and leaving enough to press the edges and seal. Repeat the procedure with the remaining sausage links and pastry. Cut the sausage rolls into bite-size pieces. Arrange on a rack in a baking pan; do not allow the edges to touch. Sprinkle with paprika. Bake for 20 to 25 minutes or until golden brown. Serve warm with the dip.

Note: You can prepare these rolls and freeze on a baking sheet. Remove to an airtight container and store in the freezer. Thaw for one hour; bake as indicated.

Diana von Welanetz Wentworth's Caviar Soufflé Appetizers

Makes 48

Soufflés

1/4 cup unsifted all-purpose flour
1 teaspoon salt
1 cup milk
3 egg yolks
4 egg whites, at room temperature
Grated zest of 1/2 lemon
2 teaspoons fresh lemon juice
Dash of Tabasco sauce
Grated fresh nutmeg to taste

Caviar Topping

6 ounces cream cheese, softened
2 tablespoons sour cream
1 teaspoon fresh lemon juice
Black caviar

Soufflés

Preheat the oven to 375 degrees. Spray forty-eight miniature muffin cups with nonstick cooking spray. Combine the flour and salt with 1/4 cup of the milk in a heavy nonstick saucepan and blend until smooth. Add the remaining 3/4 cup milk and mix well. Cook over medium heat until thickened, stirring constantly. Remove from the heat and vigorously whisk in the egg yolks. Add the lemon zest, lemon juice, Tabasco sauce and nutmeg; whisk until smooth.

Beat the eggs whites in a clean mixing bowl until soft peaks form and the whites do not slide in the bowl when it is tilted. Fold half the egg whites at a time into the cooked mixture. Spoon into the prepared muffin cups. Bake for 15 minutes or until light golden brown. Cool in the pans; the soufflés will sink slightly.

Topping

Combine the cream cheese, sour cream and lemon juice in a bowl and mix well. Spoon into a sealable plastic bag and cut off one corner. Pipe the topping onto the soufflés. Top with a tiny dollop of black caviar.

Note: You can prepare the soufflés up to one day in advance and serve at room temperature or reheat in a low oven. Remember that caviar freezes well, so you can always have it on hand.

Diana von Welanetz Wentworth is an award-winning cookbook author and television host, co-author of the best-selling Chicken Soup for the Soul Cookbook, *and author of six other cookbooks. Known for her down-home elegance, Diana hosted her own long-running daily television series. "The New Way Gourmet" aired internationally on the Lifetime Network to millions of viewers. She is also the owner of Diana's Divine Fudge and is the creator of the new Balboa Island Fudge.*

Stuffed Mushrooms

Serves 8 to 10

20 large mushroom caps
2 tablespoons olive oil
1/2 teaspoon garlic salt
8 ounces cream cheese, softened
4 ounces bacon, crisp-cooked
    and crumbled
1/2 cup (2 ounces) grated
    Parmesan cheese
1/4 cup (1 ounce) shredded
    Cheddar cheese
2 tablespoons chopped fresh parsley
2 teaspoons minced onion

Preheat the oven to 300 degrees. Combine the mushroom caps with the olive oil and garlic salt in a large sealable plastic bag and shake gently to coat the mushrooms evenly. Arrange the mushroom caps on a baking sheet.

Combine the cream cheese, bacon, Parmesan cheese, Cheddar cheese, parsley and onion in a bowl and mix well. Spoon about 1 teaspoon of the cheese mixture into each mushroom cap. Bake for 10 minutes. Serve warm.

Note: For a vegetarian appetizer, omit the bacon and add 1/3 cup gorgonzola cheese.

Scallop Baguettes

Serves 12

1 pound fresh bay scallops
3 tablespoons butter
2 tablespoons grated lemon zest
3 garlic cloves, minced
2 cups mayonnaise
2 cups (8 ounces) shredded Swiss cheese
    or Gruyère cheese
2 tablespoons chopped fresh dill weed
1 baguette, sliced 1/4 inch thick

Rinse the scallops and pat dry. Combine the scallops with the butter, lemon zest and garlic in a sauté pan. Sauté until the scallops are opaque. Remove to a bowl to cool. Add the mayonnaise, Swiss cheese and dill weed and mix gently.

Spoon the scallop mixture onto the bread slices and arrange on a broiler pan. Broil until bubbly and heated through.

Note: You can store the scallop mixture in the freezer.

Smoked Salmon on Flatbread

Serves 12 to 24

1 large flatbread or pizza crust
8 ounces cream cheese, softened
2 tablespoons capers
2 tablespoons chopped red onion
4 to 8 ounces smoked salmon
2 tablespoons chopped fresh dill weed

Preheat the oven to 400 degrees. Place the flatbread on a baking sheet and heat in the oven for 10 minutes; remove from the oven. Spread with the cream cheese and sprinkle with the capers and onion. Arrange the smoked salmon over the top and sprinkle with the dill weed. Chill for 30 minutes or longer. Cut into 3-inch portions or into wedges if using a pizza crust.

Jeff Lavia's Pesto Flatbread

Serves 27

8 ounces fresh basil leaves, torn
1/4 cup toasted pine nuts
1/4 cup (1 ounce) freshly grated
    Parmesan cheese
3 garlic cloves
Pinch of salt
Pinch of black pepper
1/8 teaspoon crushed red chili
    pepper (optional)
1/4 cup extra-virgin olive oil
9 round (6- to 8-inch) Middle Eastern
    flatbreads
3 cups (12 ounces) shredded
    fontina cheese

Combine the basil, pine nuts, Parmesan cheese, garlic, salt, black pepper and chili pepper in a food processor. Pulse several times. Add the olive oil gradually, processing constantly to form a paste. Taste and adjust the seasonings.

Preheat the oven to 400 degrees. Arrange the flatbreads on a baking sheet. Spread the pesto over the flatbread, spreading to the edges. Sprinkle evenly with the fontina cheese. Bake for 10 to 12 minutes or until the fontina cheese is melted and bubbly. Let stand for several minutes; cut each flatbread into six wedges. Serve hot or at room temperature.

Rebecca Lacko's Chicken Sausage Crostini

Makes 24

1/2 yellow onion, chopped
2 garlic cloves, minced
1 to 2 tablespoons extra-virgin olive oil
2 links chicken sausage, chopped
Splash of balsamic vinegar or red wine
1/4 cup (1 ounce) shredded fresh
    Parmesan cheese
Sea salt and cracked pepper to taste
1 large baguette, sliced into 24 rounds

Preheat the oven to 350 degrees. Stir-fry the onion and garlic in the olive oil in a medium sauté pan until tender. Add the chicken sausage and balsamic vinegar. Cook for several minutes, stirring constantly. Combine with the Parmesan cheese in a bowl and season with salt and pepper.

Arrange the baguette rounds on a baking sheet. Spoon the sausage mixture onto the rounds. Bake for 5 to 7 minutes or until bubbly. Serve immediately.

Note: For a low-carb option, you may spoon the sausage mixture into mushroom caps. Arrange the filled mushroom caps on a baking sheet and bake as directed above.

Rebecca Lacko is a food writer and family health expert living in Capistrano Beach. Her column, "The Unassuming Foodie," satisfies those of us who are truly interested in food—not just the tasting and consuming of food, but also in how different kinds of food and spices can heal, provide specific nutrients, and how they grow or earned a peculiar name. At www.UnassumingFoodie.com, you will find quirky and unexpected, yet elegant recipes suitable for a variety of diets.

Crostini with Blue Cheese, Honey and Walnuts

Makes 24

24 (1/3-inch) diagonal slices baguette
2 tablespoons olive oil
6 ounces creamy blue cheese
   or Cambozola
2/3 cup toasted coarsely chopped walnuts
1 or 2 ripe figs, thinly sliced
3 tablespoons honey, warmed

Preheat the oven to 375 degrees. Arrange the baguette slices on a baking sheet and brush with the olive oil. Toast until golden brown.

Combine the blue cheese and walnuts in a bowl and mix well. Spread evenly to the edges of the baguette slices. Bake just until the cheese melts. Arrange on a serving platter and top each with a slice of fig. Drizzle with the honey and serve warm,

Note: You can substitute dried figs for the fresh figs, adding them to the crostini before baking.

Happy Hour Toast

Makes 48

16 ounces cream cheese, softened
1 cup light mayonnaise
1 cup finely chopped green onions
5 ounces blue cheese, crumbled
1 teaspoon cayenne pepper
Grated zest of 1 lemon
1 French baguette, cut into 1/4-inch slices

Preheat the oven to 350 degrees. Spray a baking sheet with olive oil.

Combine the cream cheese, mayonnaise, green onions, blue cheese, cayenne pepper and half the lemon zest in a bowl; mix well. Spread on the baguette slices and arrange on the prepared baking sheet.

Bake the slices for 12 to 15 minute or until the topping is bubbly. Sprinkle with the remaining lemon zest and garnish with additional chopped green onions. Serve with Champagne.

Note: You can prepare the cream cheese mixture in advance and freeze it in the desired amounts in airtight containers until needed.

Blanched Asparagus with Mustard Horseradish Dip

Serves 8

1 cup sour cream
2 tablespoons whole grain mustard
1 tablespoon refrigerated grated
    fresh horseradish
1/4 teaspoon ground white pepper
1 bunch fresh asparagus, trimmed

Combine the sour cream, mustard, horseradish and white pepper in a bowl and mix well. Add the asparagus to a saucepan of boiling water and cook for up to 1 minute; drain. Plunge into ice water to stop the cooking process and preserve the bright green color. Serve with the dip and fresh lemon wedges.

Balsamic Marinated Vegetables

Serves 8

1/2 cup olive oil
1/2 cup balsamic vinegar
1 bunch basil, julienned
Salt and pepper to taste
1 red onion
1 red bell pepper
1 yellow bell pepper
1 green bell pepper
1 cucumber
1 bunch broccoli
1 package cherry tomatoes or
    grape tomatoes
1 (8-ounce) can whole black
    olives, drained

Combine the olive oil, balsamic vinegar, basil, salt and pepper in a sealable plastic bag. Cut the onion into rings. Slice the bell peppers and cucumber. Cut the broccoli into bite-size pieces. Add the cut-up vegetables, cherry tomatoes and olives to the plastic bag and turn to coat well. Marinate in the refrigerator for 4 hours or longer.

Drain the vegetables and arrange on a platter lined with lettuce leaves.

Jeff Lavia's Cocktail Turkey Florentine Meatballs with Chunky Marinara Dipping Sauce

Serves 10

Turkey Florentine Meatballs

2 tablespoons extra-virgin olive oil
1/2 cup chopped onion
1 tablespoon minced garlic
1 tablespoon chopped fresh thyme, or
    1/2 tablespoon dried thyme leaves
1 tablespoon Worcestershire sauce
1/4 cup chicken stock
Salt and pepper to taste
2 pounds ground turkey
1 (10-ounce) package frozen chopped
    spinach, thawed and drained
1/4 cup bread crumbs
1/4 cup (1 ounce) grated
    Parmesan cheese
1 egg, beaten
Olive oil for drizzling

Meatballs

Preheat the oven to 400 degrees. Drizzle 2 tablespoons olive oil into a skillet over medium heat. Add the onion, garlic and thyme. Sauté for 10 minutes or until tender but not brown. Add the Worcestershire sauce and stock and cook for several minutes. Season with salt and pepper. Cool to room temperature.

Place the turkey in a bowl and make a well in the center. Add the spinach, bread crumbs, Parmesan cheese, egg and onion mixture. Mix the ingredients, taking care not to overmix the turkey. Shape into twenty meatballs.

Arrange the meatballs on a baking sheet lined with foil. Drizzle with additional olive oil. Bake for 18 minutes or until cooked through.

Chunky Marinara Dipping Sauce

2 tablespoons extra-virgin olive oil

$1/2$ cup chopped onion

1 tablespoon minced garlic

Salt and black pepper to taste

$1/4$ teaspoon crushed red chile pepper
  (optional)

1 (28-ounce) can diced organic tomatoes
  or other good tomatoes

2 tablespoons chopped fresh basil

Sauce

Heat a saucepan over medium heat and add the olive oil, onion and garlic. Sauté for 10 minutes or until tender but not brown. Season with salt, black pepper and chile pepper. Cook for several minutes; stir in the tomatoes. Bring to a boil. Reduce the heat and simmer for 15 minutes or until reduced to a sauce consistency. Stir in the basil and remove from the heat. Serve with the meatballs, providing decorative wooden picks for dipping.

Jeff Lavia is the owner and head chef of Dinner MoJo, the region's premier personal chef service. He is a self-taught chef who takes pride in serving delicious homemade food to friends, family, and clients. Chef Jeff loves to share his passion for food and enjoys exploring Italian, French, and Mediterranean cooking styles and flavors. A frequenter of local farmers' markets, Chef Jeff believes in keeping ingredients fresh and local as much as possible.

A Restaurant's Spicy Tuna Eggplant Tempura

Makes 20

20 ounces sushi-grade tuna,
    finely chopped
1 cup mayonnaise
1/4 cup Asian chili sauce
2 cups all-purpose flour
1 cup cornstarch
3 cups soda water
Pinch of salt
1 eggplant, sliced
Vegetable oil
Chopped chives
Tobiko caviar

Combine the tuna, mayonnaise and chili sauce in a bowl and mix well. Combine the flour, cornstarch, soda water and salt in a bowl and mix well. Dip the eggplant into the batter, coating well. Deep-fry in oil in a deep skillet until golden brown.

Arrange the eggplant on a platter. Top with the tuna mixture and sprinkle with chives and caviar.

A Restaurant reflects Tim and Liza Goodell's progressive approach to fine dining: simple, delicious, updated American-style classics that exude "refined comfort food." The restaurant's former old-world flair has been maintained by its new co-owners, Hollywood director McG (Charlie's Angels; We Are Marshall) and Mark McGrath (Sugar Ray). Its speakeasy-meets-clubhouse interior invokes the 1920s, and vintage plaid carpeting and chestnut paneling take you away from its beachside location to an era of the unapologetically cool.

Spicy Baked Shrimp

Serves 10

1/2 cup olive oil
2 tablespoons fresh lemon juice
2 tablespoons chopped fresh parsley
2 tablespoons honey
2 garlic cloves, chopped
1 tablespoon soy sauce
2 tablespoons Cajun seasoning or
    Creole seasoning
1 teaspoon cayenne pepper
1 pound shrimp, peeled and deveined

Combine the olive oil, lemon juice, parsley, honey, garlic and soy sauce in a bowl and mix well. Season with the Cajun seasoning and cayenne pepper. Add the shrimp and toss to coat well. Spoon into a 9×13-inch baking dish. Marinate in the refrigerator for 1 to 2 hours.

Preheat the oven to 450 degrees. Bake the shrimp for 10 minutes or until cooked through, stirring occasionally. Spoon into a dish using a slotted spoon, reserving the marinade mixture. Serve with lemon wedges, crusty French bread and the reserved marinade for dipping.

Warm Brie with Blueberry Compote

Serves 8

1 cup fresh or frozen wild blueberries
1/4 cup packed light brown sugar
2 tablespoons cider vinegar
2 tablespoons finely chopped onion
1 1/2 teaspoons grated fresh gingerroot
1 1/2 teaspoons cornstarch
1 (3-inch) cinnamon stick
1/8 teaspoon salt
1 (12-ounce) round Brie cheese

Combine the blueberries, brown sugar, vinegar, onion, gingerroot, cornstarch, cinnamon stick and salt in a large saucepan; mix well. Bring to a boil over medium heat and cook for 1 minute, stirring frequently. Remove from the heat and discard the cinnamon stick. Cool slightly. Place, covered, in the refrigerator for 30 to 45 minutes or until completely cooled.

Preheat the oven to 350 degrees. Place the Brie cheese on an ungreased baking sheet. Bake for 10 to 12 minutes or until the cheese is softened.

Remove the cheese to a serving platter and top with the blueberry compote. Garnish with freshly cut flowering herbs and serve with bread or crackers.

Blue Cheese and Chive Brie

Serves 10 to 12

1 (15-ounce) can pitted dark cherries in
    heavy syrup
1 cup sugar
1/2 cup brandy
16 ounces cream cheese, softened
4 ounces blue cheese, crumbled
3 tablespoons mayonnaise
2 tablespoons chopped fresh chives or
    dried chives
1 round Brie cheese
1/4 cup sliced almonds, toasted

Drain the cherries, reserving the syrup. Chop the cherries and combine with the reserved syrup in a saucepan. Add the sugar and brandy and mix well. Bring to a boil over medium-high heat. Reduce the heat and simmer for 30 minutes or until reduced by about half and of a syrup consistency.

Combine the cream cheese, blue cheese, mayonnaise and chives in a bowl and mix until smooth.

Cut the Brie cheese into halves horizontally. Place the bottom half cut side up on a platter. Spread with about half the cream cheese mixture. Spread with a thin layer of the cherry mixture and sprinkle with one-third of the almonds.

Spread the remaining cream cheese mixture on the cut side of the remaining Brie half and place upright on the bottom half. Pour the remaining cherry mixture over the top and sprinkle with the remaining almonds.

Place the Brie in the refrigerator and chill for 8 hours or longer. Let stand at room temperature for 1 hour before serving. Serve with crackers.

Cathy Thomas's Pesto Appetizer Loaf

Serves 24

Basil Cream Cheese

1 large garlic clove
1/2 cup fresh basil leaves
16 ounces cream cheese, softened
Salt and pepper to taste

Pesto

2 large garlic cloves
1 1/2 cups fresh basil leaves
1 cup (4 ounces) grated Parmesan cheese
1/3 cup extra-virgin olive oil

Appetizer Loaf

1/3 cup pine nuts
16 ounces provolone cheese, thinly
    sliced lengthwise
1/2 cup oil-pack sun-dried tomatoes,
    drained and cut into thin strips

Basil Cream Cheese

Process the garlic and basil leaves in a food processor fitted with a metal blade until minced. Add the cream cheese and process until smooth. Season with salt and pepper and process until blended. Remove to a bowl.

Pesto

Process the garlic and basil in the food processor until minced. Add the Parmesan cheese and process until smooth. Add the olive oil gradually, processing constantly until blended.

Appetizer Loaf

Preheat the oven to 350 degrees. Spread the pine nuts in a single layer on a baking sheet. Place on the center oven rack and toast for 2 minutes. Shake the pan to turn the pine nuts and toast for 1 minute longer or until light brown; watch carefully to avoid burning.

Moisten a 16×16-inch cheesecloth with cold water and squeeze out the excess water. Line a 4 1/2×8 1/2-inch loaf pan with the cloth, allowing the extra cloth to extend over the sides.

Line the prepared loaf pan completely with about half the provolone cheese slices, overlapping the edges, pressing down the seams and allowing the edges of the cheese to hang over the sides of the loaf pan.

Spread about half the basil cream cheese in the prepared loaf pan, pressing into an even layer. Arrange the sun-dried tomatoes over the cream cheese and press down lightly. Top with a layer of the remaining provolone cheese. Spread half the pesto over the provolone cheese and add another layer of provolone cheese.

Pesto Appetizer Loaf continued

Spread with the remaining cream cheese and top with the toasted pine nuts, pushing the pine nuts down lightly. Finish with a layer of provolone cheese, the remaining pesto mixture and the remaining provolone cheese.

Fold the excess provolone cheese over the layers. Fold the edges of the cheesecloth over the top of the loaf and press down gently. Cover with plastic wrap and chill for 2 hours. Remove the plastic wrap and unfold the cheesecloth from the top. Invert onto a dark-colored serving platter and remove the cheesecloth. Garnish with sprigs of fresh basil and pesticide-free edible flowers. Serve with French bread or crackers.

Note: You can substitute two (7-ounce) containers of prepared refrigerator pesto and two (8-ounce) containers of spreadable cheese with garlic and herbs for the spreads in this recipe if you prefer. Remember to drain the excess oil from the prepared pesto. You can also store the loaf in an airtight container in the refrigerator for up to 4 days or in the freezer for up to 2 months.

Orange County Register *food columnist Cathy Thomas thinks cooking is fun. She pioneered the use of culinary-based flash videos on the Web. To make cooking more pleasurable for her readers, she filmed hundreds of cooking "how-tos" and celebrity interviews for the newspaper's Web site, www.ocregister.com.food. She is the author of Melissa's Great Book of Produce.*

Herbed Goat Cheese with Sourdough Toasts

Serves 6

8 chive stems
Leaves of 2 sprigs fresh rosemary
1/4 cup parsley leaves
Coarsely ground pepper to taste
1 (8-ounce) log goat cheese
1 sourdough baguette
Extra-virgin olive oil

Combine the chives, rosemary and parsley in a food processor and process just until chopped. Combine with the pepper on a sheet of waxed paper. Roll the goat cheese in the herbs, coating evenly. Wrap in the waxed paper and chill in the refrigerator.

Preheat the oven to 350 degrees. Slice the baguette diagonally 1/4 inch thick. Arrange the slices on a baking sheet and brush with olive oil. Bake for several minutes or until lightly toasted.

Place the goat cheese in the center of a serving platter and garnish with additional herbs. Arrange the warm sourdough toasts around the cheese.

Lemony Hummus

Serves 12

1 large garlic clove
2 cups canned garbanzo beans, drained
1/2 cup fresh lemon juice
1/2 cup tahini
1 teaspoon ground cumin
1 3/4 teaspoons salt
1/2 cup olive oil
1 teaspoon extra-virgin olive oil
3 pinches of paprika

Process the garlic in a food processor until minced. Add the garbanzo beans and lemon juice. Process until creamy, scraping the side of the processor bowl as needed. Add the tahini, cumin and salt and process until smooth. Add 1/2 cup olive oil and process until blended. Spoon into a serving bowl and drizzle with 1 teaspoon olive oil. Sprinkle with the paprika.

Shrimp Spread

Serves 20

2 cups cooked fresh shrimp, or
    2 (6-ounce) cans shrimp, drained
8 ounces cream cheese, softened
2 tablespoons butter
2 tablespoons mayonnaise
Juice of 1 lemon
1 small onion, chopped
Garlic salt, salt and pepper to taste

Chop the shrimp in a food processor; set aside. Combine the cream cheese with the butter, mayonnaise, lemon juice, onion, garlic salt, salt and pepper in a food processor or mixing bowl. Process or beat until smooth. Add the shrimp and process to mix well. Serve with crackers.

Cranberry Orange Spread

Serves 12

8 ounces cream cheese, softened
2 tablespoons thawed frozen orange
    juice concentrate
1 tablespoon sugar
Grated zest of 1 orange
$1/8$ teaspoon cinnamon
$1/4$ cup dried cranberries,
    finely chopped
$1/4$ cup pecans, finely chopped
    (optional)

Combine the cream cheese, orange juice concentrate, sugar, orange zest and cinnamon in a medium mixing bowl. Beat at medium speed until smooth and fluffy. Stir in the cranberries and pecans. Chill for 1 hour or longer. Serve with crackers.

Spicy Artichoke Jalapeño Dip

Serves 8 to 10

1 (14-ounce) can artichoke hearts in water
1 (4-ounce) can chopped jalapeño chiles
8 ounces Parmesan cheese, grated
1 cup mayonnaise
1 cup sour cream

Preheat the oven to 350 degrees. Drain and chop the artichoke hearts. Drain the jalapeño chiles. Combine the artichoke hearts, jalapeño chiles, Parmesan cheese, mayonnaise and sour cream in a bowl and mix well. Spoon into an 8×8-inch baking dish and bake for 20 to 25 minutes or until golden brown and bubby. Serve with crackers or sliced French baguette.

Chef Jamie Gwen's Reuben Dip

Serves 12

8 ounces cream cheese, softened
1 cup (4 ounces) shredded Swiss cheese
3/4 cup Thousand Island salad dressing
1 1/2 cups chopped corned beef
1 cup rinsed drained sauerkraut
1 cup (4 ounces) shredded Swiss cheese
1/4 cup (1 ounce) grated Parmesan cheese

Preheat the oven to 375 degrees. Combine the cream cheese and 1 cup Swiss cheese in a mixing bowl and mix well. Spread in the bottom of a 9-inch pie plate. Drizzle with half the salad dressing. Layer the corned beef and sauerkraut in the prepared plate and drizzle with the remaining salad dressing. Top with 1 cup Swiss cheese and Parmesan cheese. Bake for 20 to 25 minutes or until the mixture begins to bubble and the cheese melts.

As a chef, food correspondent, sommelier, and lifestyle expert, Chef Jamie whips up delicious recipes and culinary delights for television and radio audiences around the globe. She has a weekly live radio show called "Food & Wine with Chef Jamie Gwen," and is also Celebrity Guest Chef on the Home Shopping Network. In addition, she brings her culinary and writing expertise to OC Family Magazine with her monthly recipe column. According to Chef Jamie, "Simply said, we love Reuben sandwiches...and this is the ultimate dip! Served hot and bubbling with cheese, it has everything you love about a Reuben. Serve it with cocktail rye bread for dipping and lots of napkins!"

Warm Blue Cheese and Bacon Dip

Makes 1 1/2 cups

7 slices bacon, chopped
2 garlic cloves, minced
8 ounces cream cheese, softened
1/4 cup half-and-half
4 ounces blue cheese, crumbled
2 tablespoons chopped fresh chives
3 tablespoons chopped smoked almonds

Preheat the oven to 350 degrees. Cook the bacon in a skillet over medium-high heat until almost crisp; drain the drippings. Add the garlic to the skillet and cook until the bacon is crisp.

Beat the cream cheese in a mixing bowl until smooth. Beat in the half-and-half. Stir in the bacon mixture, blue cheese and chives.

Spoon into a 2-cup baking dish. Bake, covered with foil, for 30 minutes or until heated through. Sprinkle with the almonds and serve hot with crackers, bread cubes or carrot and celery sticks.

Brie Bruschetta Dip

Serves 8 to 10

1 (17-ounce) round Brie cheese
4 Roma tomatoes, seeded and
    finely chopped
1 cup fresh basil, chopped
2 garlic cloves, minced
1/4 cup olive oil
Salt and freshly ground pepper to taste
1 French baguette

Preheat the oven to 350 degrees. Trim the rind from the Brie cheese and chop the cheese into very small pieces. Combine with the tomatoes, basil, garlic, olive oil, salt and pepper in a bowl; mix well.

Slice the baguette and arrange on a baking sheet. Bake just until toasted. Serve with the dip.

Chef Jamie Gwen's Caramelized Onion Dip

Makes 2 cups

2 tablespoons extra-virgin olive oil

2 tablespoons unsalted butter

2 large yellow onions, cut into halves and
   thinly sliced

Salt and white pepper to taste

2 tablespoons dry white wine or
   chicken broth

1/2 cup sour cream

1/2 cup mayonnaise

4 ounces whipped cream cheese

Heat the olive oil and butter in a sauté pan over medium heat. Add the onions and sauté for 10 minutes, stirring frequently. Season with salt and white pepper. Reduce the heat to low and cook for 20 minutes or until the onions are golden brown and caramelized. Increase the heat to medium and add the wine, stirring up the brown bits from the bottom of the skillet. Remove from the heat and cool to room temperature.

Combine the sour cream, mayonnaise and cream cheese in a large mixing bowl and beat until smooth. Add the caramelized onions and mix well. Adjust the seasoning and serve at room temperature. Serve with chips, vegetables or pretzels.

This recipe was excerpted from Good Food for Good Times *by Jamie Gwen with Lana Sills. Chef Jamie tells us that this is better than any onion dip you've ever had...sweet, creamy, and the real thing! The secret to the caramelized flavor is to slowly cook the onions until they are sweet and golden brown.*

Avocado Feta Dip

Serves 6

2 tomatoes, chopped
1 avocado, chopped
6 ounces feta cheese, crumbled
1/4 cup chopped red onion
1 garlic clove, minced
1 tablespoon chopped parsley
1 tablespoon olive oil
1 tablespoon white wine vinegar
Chopped jalapeño chiles to taste
Red pepper flakes to taste
Oregano, salt and pepper to taste

Combine the tomatoes, avocado, feta cheese, onion, garlic and parsley in a bowl. Add the olive oil and wine vinegar and mix gently. Stir in jalapeño chiles and red pepper. Season with oregano, salt and pepper. Place the avocado pit in the bowl until ready to serve to keep the avocado from turning brown.

Guacamole

Serves 12 to 15

6 Roma tomatoes, coarsely chopped
1 cup chopped onion
6 garlic cloves, minced
1 cup cilantro, chopped
2 jalapeño chiles, seeded and chopped
Juice of 1 lime
1 teaspoon kosher salt
1/4 teaspoon cayenne pepper, or to taste
1/2 teaspoon freshly ground black pepper
9 avocados, coarsely chopped

Combine the tomatoes, onion, garlic, cilantro and jalapeño chiles in a bowl. Add the lime juice, kosher salt, cayenne pepper and black pepper and mix well. Add the avocado and mix gently. Serve with tortilla chips or on a salad.

Shrimp Salsa

Serves 8 to 10

12 limes
1¹/₂ pounds peeled large shrimp, chopped
1 (16-ounce) can diced tomatoes
2 bunches green onions, chopped
1 bunch cilantro, chopped
¹/₂ cup ketchup
4 or 5 avocados, sliced and chopped

Squeeze the lime and measure the juice. Combine the juice with an equal amount of water in a bowl and mix well. Let stand for 1 hour or longer.

Combine the shrimp with the tomato, green onions and cilantro in a bowl. Add the lime juice mixture and ketchup and mix well. Marinate in the refrigerator for 8 hours or longer to cook the shrimp in the lime juice. Add the avocados 1 hour before serving and mix gently.

Chunky Salsa

Serves 10

4 tomatoes, chopped
¹/₂ cup chopped onion
¹/₂ cup chopped celery
¹/₄ cup chopped green bell pepper
¹/₃ (4-ounce) can chopped green
    chiles, drained
¹/₄ cup vegetable oil
2 tablespoons wine vinegar
1 teaspoon mustard seeds
1 teaspoon crushed coriander seeds
2 dashes of ground cumin
1 dash of garlic powder
1 teaspoon salt
1 dash of pepper

Combine the tomatoes, onion, celery, bell pepper and green chiles in a bowl. Add the oil and wine vinegar; mix well. Add the mustard seeds, coriander, cumin, garlic powder, salt and pepper and mix well. Chill for 1 hour or longer. Serve with chips.

Orange Cilantro Salsa

Makes 2 cups

4 oranges, peeled, sectioned and chopped
1 bunch cilantro, chopped
1 small red onion, julienned
1 small jalapeño chile, seeded and
    finely chopped
10 sprigs of mint, torn
1/4 cup olive oil
1/4 cup red wine vinegar
Juice of 1 large lime
1 teaspoon salt
1/2 teaspoon pepper

Combine the oranges, cilantro, onion, jalapeño chile and mint in a bowl. Add the olive oil, wine vinegar and lime juice. Season with salt and pepper and mix well. Serve with corn chips or as an accompaniment for chicken or shrimp.

A Restaurant's Cucumber Cooler

Serves 1

8 to 10 cucumber slices
1/2 teaspoon yuzu juice
3 or 4 sprigs of basil
1/2 ounce simple syrup
1 1/2 ounces gin
3/4 ounce sweet-and-sour mix
Ginger ale

Combine the cucumber, yuzu juice, basil and simple syrup in a cocktail shaker and muddle to blend the flavors. Add the gin, sweet-and-sour mix and ice and close the shaker. Shake and roll to mix well and distribute the cucumber and basil. Pour into a glass and top with ginger ale.

The Perfect Margarita

Serves 2

Simple Syrup

1 cup sugar

4 to 5 cups water

Perfect Margarita

2 cups crushed ice

3 ounces silver tequila

2 ounces brandy

2 ounces orange liqueur

Juice of 2 limes

Simple Syrup

Combine the sugar with the water in a saucepan and bring to a boil. Boil until the sugar dissolves, stirring constantly. Remove from the heat and cool completely.

Margarita

Place two martini glasses in the freezer for 10 minutes. Combine the crushed ice with 3/4 cup of the simple syrup, the tequila, brandy, orange liqueur and lime juice in a shaker. Close the shaker and shake for 30 seconds. Strain into the chilled martini glasses and serve.

The southern California coastal plain, including what is now Orange County, was home to many Native Americans. The Gabrielinos who lived here had access to fertile land and the sea, so they had a more abundant lifestyle.

Zingin' Margaritas

Serves 6 to 8

1 (12-ounce) can frozen limeade
    concentrate, thawed
3 cups water
12 ounces silver or gold tequila
6 ounces light Mexican beer
6 ounces Triple Sec
3 ounces Cointreau
3 cups crushed ice

Combine the limeade concentrate, water, tequila, beer and orange liqueurs in a large pitcher and mix gently. Serve over the crushed ice in glasses with salted rims. Garnish with lime wedges.

Fresh Strawberry Shakes

Serves 2

2 cups whole strawberries
1/4 cup sweetened condensed milk
1/2 cup coconut milk
1 cup crushed ice

Combine the strawberries with the sweetened condensed milk, coconut milk and crushed ice in a blender and blend until smooth. Serve immediately in chilled glasses. You can substitute bananas, pineapple or other fruit for the strawberries.

Disneyland's Blue Bayou Mint Julep

Makes 10 quarts

1 (1-pound) package sugar

6 cups water

1$\frac{1}{4}$ ounces thawed lime juice
concentrate

8$\frac{1}{2}$ ounces thawed lemonade
concentrate

$\frac{3}{4}$ cup crème de menthe syrup

Combine the sugar and water in a 3-quart saucepan. Heat until the sugar dissolves completely, stirring constantly. Stir in the lime juice concentrate and lemonade concentrate. Add the crème de menthe syrup. Cook to just below the boiling point, 210 degrees; do not allow to boil. Chill in the refrigerator. Dilute with 5 parts chilled water to 1 part syrup to serve.

At Disneyland's Blue Bayou Restaurant, savor down-home Louisiana-inspired cooking and full table service in a moonlit ambiance as Pirates of the Caribbean passenger boats drift past. This popular restaurant serves a range of delectable dishes for lunch and dinner at the happiest place on Earth.

California Fresh

SIDE DISHES

Before fancy malls and planned communities became the face of Orange County, the region was dominated by farmland, in particular, orange groves. In 1889 Orange County successfully broke away from the County of Los Angeles to become its own political entity. Farming became the most important industry in the county as Valencia oranges, lemons, avocados, and walnuts were harvested year-round. With oranges taking over as the main crop, the region was named for the fruit.

As the years passed, a transformation began in Orange County—oil was discovered in Huntington Beach; the birth of the aerospace industry took place on the Irvine Ranch; and Hollywood found its way to The OC, filming several classics in the Newport Beach area. With neighboring Los Angeles growing rapidly, the more laid-back lifestyle and better cost of living made Orange County an attractive place to live. By the 1960s the population in Orange County was booming, and with the massive influx of residents came an urban landscape of homes, shopping malls, and industrial parks.

Though farming is no longer the main industry in Orange County, fresh California produce is still a main staple in Orange County kitchens. Almost every day of the week a farmers' market is held in one of the Orange County cities at which patrons can purchase fresh, locally grown produce direct from the farmer.

SWEET
PEACHES
$2.50 lb.
NO PESTICIDES

WATERMELONS
$

Spring Salad

Serves 6 to 8

1/4 cup olive oil
2 tablespoons balsamic vinegar
2 dashes of Tabasco sauce
2 tablespoons sugar, or an equivalent
    amount of artificial sweetener
1 tablespoon parsley flakes
1/2 teaspoon salt
1/2 teaspoon pepper
2 packages romaine or spring lettuce mix
1 (16-ounce) container fresh
    strawberries, sliced
1 cup (4 ounces) shredded extra-aged
    white Cheddar cheese
1/4 cup caramelized pecans

Combine the olive oil, balsamic vinegar, Tabasco sauce, sugar, parsley flakes, salt and pepper in a bowl and whisk to mix well.

Combine the lettuce with the strawberries, Cheddar cheese and pecans in a salad bowl. Add the dressing and toss lightly to coat evenly.

Colorful Salad

Serves 3

1 package romaine
1 cup chopped strawberries
1/2 cup golden raisins
1/2 cup sunflower seeds
1 (15-ounce) can mandarin
    oranges, drained
8 ounces cooked crab meat or
    chopped cooked chicken
Poppy seed dressing to taste

Spread the lettuce on serving plates. Top with the strawberries, raisins, sunflower seeds and mandarin oranges. Top the salads evenly with the crab meat. Chill until serving time. Drizzle with salad dressing and serve with blueberry muffins.

Richard Nixon's Snowball Salad

Serves 4 to 6

3 pears, peeled
4 heads Bibb lettuce
3 oranges, peeled and sectioned
12 large strawberries
24 black cherries, pitted
1 pint lemon sorbet
1/4 cup shredded coconut

Cut each pear into six wedges. Line serving plates with the lettuce leaves. Arrange the pears, oranges, strawberries and cherries alternately in a circular pattern around the plates, leaving the centers open. Scoop the lemon sorbet into the centers of the plates. Sprinkle with the coconut and serve immediately.

Note: To use fresh coconut, warm a whole coconut in a 350-degree oven for 20 to 30 minutes to soften the shell. Pierce through one of the "eyes" with an ice pick or screwdriver and drain, reserving the milk for sauces or drinks. Crack the shell by tapping gently with a hammer and pare the coconut from the shell. Grate the coconut and toast lightly, if desired. The flavor of the fresh coconut is well worth the extra effort.

The Richard Nixon Library and Birthplace is a nonprofit institution dedicated to educating the public about the life and times of the thirty-seventh president and encouraging interest in history, government, and public affairs. The most active, innovative, and visited presidential center in America, it conducts a wide range of public affairs programming, ranging from town meetings to an impressive roster of distinguished speakers. Richard Nixon was born in Yorba Linda.

Asian Chopped Salad

Serves 6 to 8

1/4 cup lemon juice

1/4 cup vegetable oil

3 tablespoons soy sauce

2 tablespoons white vinegar

2 tablespoons dark brown sugar

1 tablespoon freshly grated
    gingerroot

2 teaspoons sesame oil

1 teaspoon salt

1/2 teaspoon pepper

1 head cabbage, finely chopped

1/2 bunch scallions, trimmed and
    thinly sliced

1 cup julienned carrots

1/2 cup crisp won ton strips or chow
    mein noodles

1/2 cup peanuts

2 teaspoons sesame seeds

Combine the lemon juice, vegetable oil, soy sauce, white vinegar, brown sugar, gingerroot, sesame oil, salt and pepper in a bowl and mix well.

Toss the cabbage with the scallions and carrots in a large bowl. Add the dressing at serving time and toss to coat well. Sprinkle with the won ton strips, peanuts and sesame seeds. Serve within 30 minutes to ensure that the cabbage will remain crisp.

Hearts of Palm Salad

Serves 4

Tangy Dressing
1/2 cup olive oil
1 egg
2 teaspoons Worcestershire sauce
2 teaspoons garlic salt
1 tablespoon lemon pepper
Juice of 1 or 2 fresh lemons

Hearts of Palm Salad
1 bunch spinach
1 head romaine, torn
1 (14-ounce) can hearts of palm,
    drained and chopped
1/4 cup finely chopped red onion
8 slices bacon, crisp-cooked and
    crumbled (optional)
1/2 cup (2 ounces) grated
    Parmesan cheese
1 cup crumbled breadsticks

Dressing
Combine the olive oil and egg in a small bowl and whisk until well mixed. Add the Worcestershire sauce, garlic salt and lemon pepper. Whisk in the lemon juice. Store in the refrigerator for up to 5 days.

Salad
Combine the spinach, romaine, hearts of palm, onion, bacon and Parmesan cheese in a serving bowl. Add the crumbled breadsticks at serving time and serve with the dressing.

Note: Although the lemon juice will "cook" the dressing and turn it white, you may be concerned about using uncooked eggs. You can substitute eggs pasteurized in their shells, which are sold at some specialty stores, or use an equivalent amount of pasteurized egg substitute.

Spinach Salad with Tortellini

Serves 4 to 6

Curried Salad Dressing

2/3 cup vegetable oil

1/4 cup red wine vinegar

2 teaspoons lemon juice

2 teaspoons soy sauce

1 1/2 teaspoons sugar

1 teaspoon dry mustard

1/2 teaspoon curry powder

1/4 teaspoon garlic powder

1 1/2 teaspoons salt

1/2 teaspoon pepper

Spinach Salad with Tortellini

8 ounces uncooked tortellini

12 ounces fresh spinach

1 (6-ounce) package dried cranberries

1/2 cup pine nuts

1/2 cup crumbled feta cheese

Dressing

Combine the oil, wine vinegar, lemon juice and soy sauce in a jar with a tight-fitting lid. Add the sugar, dry mustard, curry powder, garlic powder, salt and pepper and shake until blended.

Salad

Cook the pasta using the package directions; drain. Rinse with cold water until cool and drain again. Combine with the spinach, cranberries, pine nuts and feta cheese in a large salad bowl. Add the salad dressing and toss to coat well.

Spicy Shrimp and Tangelo Salad

Serves 4

Honey Citrus Dressing

1/4 cup extra-virgin olive oil
Juice of 1/2 tangelo
Juice of 1/2 lemon
2 tablespoons honey mustard
2 teaspoons honey
1 teaspoon grated tangelo zest
1 teaspoon grated lemon zest
1/2 teaspoon salt
1/2 teaspoon pepper

Spicy Shrimp and Tangelo

16 large shrimp, peeled, deveined and
    tails removed
2 tablespoons extra-virgin olive oil
1 tablespoon spicy steak seasoning
1 package baby spinach
1/2 cup thinly sliced red onion
Sections of 1 tangelo
1/4 cup almonds, sliced and toasted

Dressing

Combine the olive oil, tangelo juice, lemon juice, honey mustard, honey, tangelo zest, lemon zest, salt and pepper in a jar with a tight-fitting lid. Shake to mix well.

Salad

Place the shrimp in a large bowl. Drizzle with the olive oil and sprinkle with the seasoning; toss to mix well. Let stand for several minutes. Combine the spinach, onion, tangelo sections and almonds in a salad bowl.

Heat a large sauté pan over medium-high heat and add the shrimp. Sauté for 3 to 5 minutes or until opaque and cooked through. Add to the salad. Drizzle with the dressing and toss to coat well.

Vegetable Shrimp Salad

Serves 8

Lemon Dijon Dressing

1/3 cup fresh lemon juice
2 teaspoons Dijon mustard
1/2 teaspoon kosher salt
1/2 teaspoon freshly ground pepper
3/4 cup extra-virgin olive oil

Vegetable Shrimp Salad

2 pounds medium shrimp, peeled
    and cooked
1 yellow bell pepper, thinly sliced
1 small white onion, thinly sliced
1 pound green beans, cooked and
    cut into 1-inch pieces
1 cucumber, peeled and sliced
    1/4 inch thick
1/2 pint grape tomatoes, cut into halves
1/2 cup chopped celery
1 cup black olives, cut into halves
1/2 cup fresh basil leaves, chopped
1 bunch chives, thinly sliced
Lemon juice, kosher salt and pepper
    to taste

Dressing

Combine the lemon juice, Dijon mustard, kosher salt and pepper in a small bowl; whisk to mix well. Add the olive oil gradually, whisking constantly to emulsify.

Salad

Combine half the dressing with the shrimp in a bowl; toss to coat evenly. Marinate, covered, in the refrigerator for 2 hours or longer.

Combine the remaining dressing with the bell pepper, onion, green beans, cucumber, grape tomatoes, celery, black olives, basil and chives in a large bowl; toss to coat evenly. Marinate, covered, in the refrigerator.

Combine the shrimp and the vegetables in a salad bowl and mix gently. Chill for 30 minutes before serving. Adjust the seasoning with lemon juice, kosher salt and pepper as needed.

Arugula Steak Salad

Serves 8

1/2 cup canola oil
1/2 cup soy sauce
1/4 cup red wine vinegar
1/4 cup fresh lemon juice
2 tablespoons Worcestershire sauce
4 garlic cloves, thinly sliced
1 tablespoon chopped Italian parsley
1 tablespoon dry mustard, or
    2 tablespoons Dijon mustard
1/2 teaspoon kosher salt
1 teaspoon freshly ground pepper
1 (16-ounce) flank steak
5 ounces arugula
Olive oil
Vinegar

Combine the canola oil, soy sauce, wine vinegar, lemon juice, Worcestershire sauce, garlic, parsley, dry mustard, kosher salt and pepper in a bowl and whisk to mix well. Combine with the steak in a sealable plastic bag, turning to coat evenly. Marinate in the refrigerator for 6 hours to 2 days.

Preheat a grill. Drain the steak, discarding the marinade. Place the steak on the grill and grill for about 10 minutes on each side or until it feels like the fleshy part of the palm when gently pressed; do not overcook.

Cover the steak with foil and let stand for 10 to 15 minutes. Slice very thinly across the grain with a sharp carving knife. Line the serving plates with the arugula and arrange the steak slices over the arugula. Drizzle with olive oil and vinegar.

Note: Serve this salad as a main dish with a green vegetable, wild rice or potatoes, and crusty bread. For a healthier version, serve it as a salad over a beautiful bed of greens tossed lightly with a vinaigrette. Add grape tomato halves; crumbled feta or blue cheese; pepitas, pecans, or sliced almonds; dried cranberries, grape halves, chopped apples, or chopped pears; and top it with a few slices of the steak.

The Golden Truffle's Artichoke Chicken Salad

Serves 4

Avocado Ranch Dressing

1 avocado

2 cups mayonnaise

2 cups buttermilk

2 tablespoons onion powder

1 tablespoon garlic powder

1 pinch of MSG

2 teaspoons seasoning salt

1 teaspoon celery salt

3 pinches of cayenne pepper

1 teaspoon freshly ground black pepper

Artichoke Chicken Salad

4 fresh artichokes

Salt to taste

4 slices tomato

2 chicken breasts, cooked, chilled and
   sliced diagonally

1 pound asparagus, cooked, chilled
   and chopped

Dressing

Mash the avocado in a bowl. Combine with the mayonnaise, buttermilk, onion powder, garlic powder, MSG, seasoning salt, celery salt, cayenne pepper and black pepper in a blender; process until combined.

Salad

Place the artichokes in a large saucepan with enough salted water to cover. Cook until tender; drain and chill. Remove the chokes from the artichokes, leaving the leaves and exposed hearts.

Place the artichokes on serving plates and press the leaves to fan them out, leaving them still attached. Place a tomato slice on the exposed hearts and top with the chicken. Add a generous scoop of the salad dressing and sprinkle with chopped asparagus.

54

California Chicken Salad

Serves 4

1 bunch red leaf lettuce, chopped
1 (11-ounce) can mandarin
    oranges, drained
2 green onions, chopped
1 carrot, julienned or shredded
1 1/2 cups chopped cooked chicken
1 avocado, chopped
1 cup cashew pieces
2 cups crisp chow mein noodles
Poppy seed salad dressing or Asian salad
    dressing to taste
Toasted sesame seeds to taste

Combine the lettuce, mandarin oranges, green onions and carrot in a large salad bowl. Add the chicken, avocado and cashews and mix lightly. Add the noodles and salad dressing just before serving; toss to coat evenly. Top with toasted sesame seeds.

Chicken and Apricot Pita

Serves 4

1/4 cup whole almonds
1 boneless skinless chicken breast, cooked
    without salt and sliced
1/2 cup dried apricot quarters
1 rib celery, chopped
2 tablespoons chopped fresh cilantro
1/2 cup fat-free plain yogurt
1 tablespoon Dijon mustard
1 teaspoon honey
1 teaspoon grated orange zest
2 whole wheat pita rounds,
    cut into halves

Preheat the oven to 300 degrees. Spread the almonds on a baking sheet. Bake for 7 to 8 minutes or until toasted. Cool to room temperature.

Combine the almonds with the chicken, apricots, celery and cilantro in a bowl. Add the yogurt, Dijon mustard, honey and orange zest and mix well. Spoon into the pita halves to serve.

Note: You may also serve the chicken salad with mixed greens.

Chicken Corn Salad

Serves 6 to 8

6 ears fresh corn
3 tablespoons butter
2 chicken breasts, cooked
    and chopped
1 (15-ounce) can black beans,
    drained
1 cup cherry tomatoes, chopped
1/2 cup chopped red onion
1/2 cup chopped red bell pepper
1/2 cup cilantro, chopped
5 tablespoons olive oil
1/4 cup cider vinegar
1/3 cup fresh lime juice
1 teaspoon freshly ground pepper
1 avocado, chopped

Cut off the tops of the corn kernels into a bowl using a sharp knife. Heat 1 tablespoon of the butter in a large skillet over medium heat. Add one-third of the corn kernels and sauté for 1 minute, stirring constantly; do not overcook. Repeat the process two more times with the remaining butter and corn kernels.

Combine the corn with the chicken, black beans, cherry tomatoes, onion, bell pepper and cilantro in a bowl. Add the olive oil, cider vinegar, lime juice and pepper; toss to mix well. Top with the avocado at serving time. Serve chilled or at room temperature.

Note: You can omit the chicken for a vegetarian salad or substitute bacon for the chicken.

Corn is best from July to September, and white corn has the best flavor. Purchase it from your local farmers' market to ensure that you are getting the freshest and tastiest corn.

Southwest Chicken Salad

Serves 8

Southwest Salad Dressing

3/4 cup olive oil

3 tablespoons lime juice

1/2 cup chopped cilantro

4 scallions, sliced

1 tablespoon minced chipotle chile

1 tablespoon cayenne pepper or
    ground cumin

Southwest Chicken Salad

4 chicken breasts

4 ears of corn, shucked

2 poblano chiles, cut into quarters

2 red bell peppers, cut into quarters

2 cups uncooked brown rice

4 cups water

1/4 cup chopped cilantro

Dressing

    Combine the olive oil, lime juice, cilantro, scallions, chipotle chile and cayenne pepper in a bowl and whisk to mix well.

Salad

    Place the chicken, corn, poblano chiles and bell peppers on a rimmed baking sheet. Brush with 1/2 cup of the salad dressing. Let stand for 30 minutes.

    Preheat the broiler. Cook the rice in the water in a saucepan using the package directions. Spoon into a large bowl.

    Broil the chicken and vegetables until the chicken is cooked through and the vegetables are tender and slightly charred. Cut the corn kernels from the cobs using a sharp knife. Add to the rice. Cut the chicken, chiles and bell peppers into bite-size pieces. Add to the rice and mix well.

    Add the remaining salad dressing and the cilantro to the chicken mixture and toss to coat evenly.

Tarragon Chicken Salad

Serves 4 to 6

1/2 cup pecans, chopped
3 pounds boneless skinless
     chicken breasts
1 cup crème fraîche or heavy cream
2/3 cup sour cream
1/2 cup mayonnaise
2 ribs celery, cut into small strips
1 tablespoon crushed fresh
     tarragon leaves
Salt and pepper to taste

Preheat the oven to 350 degrees. Sprinkle the pecans on a baking sheet. Toast for 5 minutes.

Arrange the chicken breasts in a single layer on a large rimmed baking sheet. Spread evenly with the crème fraîche. Bake for 20 to 25 minutes or until cooked through. Cool to room temperature. Chop or shred the chicken into bite-size pieces. Place in a large salad bowl.

Combine the sour cream and mayonnaise in a small bowl and whisk until combined. Add to the chicken and toss to coat well. Add the celery, pecans, tarragon, salt and pepper and mix well.

Chill, covered, for 4 hours or longer. Adjust the seasonings before serving.

Note: For a fruity variation, add 1 1/2 cups grapes, cherries, or cranberries. Reserve the cooking juices from the baking sheet to enrich soups or sauces.

Wild Rice Chicken Salad

Serves 12

Dijon Vinaigrette

1/3 cup extra-virgin olive oil

1/4 cup wine vinegar

2 tablespoons Dijon mustard

3 garlic cloves, minced

1/2 teaspoon kosher salt

1/2 teaspoon freshly ground pepper

Wild Rice Chicken Salad

2 tablespoons fresh lemon juice

4 cups cooked wild rice

2 chicken breasts, cooked and shredded

4 green onions or scallions, sliced

1 red bell pepper, chopped

2 ounces snow peas, sliced

2 avocados, coarsely chopped

1 cup pecans halves, toasted

Vinaigrette

Combine the olive oil, wine vinegar, Dijon mustard, garlic, kosher salt and pepper in a blender and process until smooth.

Salad

Drizzle the lemon juice over the wild rice in a large bowl; let stand until cool. Add the chicken, green onions, bell pepper and snow peas. Add the vinaigrette and toss to mix well. Chill, covered, for 1 hour or up to 2 days. Add the avocados and pecans at serving time.

In 1769 Gaspar de Portola led an expedition north through California. While in Orange County, they were very frightened by several earthquakes in one day, so they named the river where they were camped the Santa Ana River, after St. Anne.

Chicken and Orzo Salad

Serves 6

16 ounces uncooked orzo
1 tablespoon salt
Olive oil
1/2 cup fresh lemon juice
    (about 3 lemons)
1/2 cup extra-virgin olive oil
1 teaspoon kosher salt
1 teaspoon pepper
1 pound skinless chicken tenders,
    cut into bite-size pieces
Salt and pepper to taste
1 pint grape tomatoes, whole or
    cut into halves if large
1 hothouse cucumber, coarsely chopped
1/2 cup finely chopped red onion
1 cup minced scallions (green and
    white portions)
1 cup chopped fresh dill weed
1 cup chopped fresh flat-leaf parsley
1 teaspoon kosher salt, or to taste
1 teaspoon pepper
12 ounces feta cheese, coarsely chopped

Bring a large saucepan of water to a boil; add the pasta, 1 tablespoon salt and a splash of olive oil. Reduce the heat and simmer for 9 to 11 minutes or until the pasta is cooked al dente; drain and place in a bowl.

Combine the lemon juice, 1/2 cup olive oil, 1 teaspoon kosher salt and 1 teaspoon pepper in a small bowl; whisk to mix well. Add to the pasta and toss to coat evenly.

Pour a small amount of olive oil into a skillet and heat over medium heat. Add the chicken and season with salt and pepper. Sauté until cooked through and light brown. Add to the pasta and mix well.

Add the grape tomatoes, cucumber, onion, scallions, dill weed, parsley, 1 teaspoon kosher salt and 1 teaspoon pepper; toss to mix well. Add the feta cheese and mix gently. Let stand at room temperature for 1 hour to blend the flavors or chill in the refrigerator for 8 hours or longer. Let chilled salad stand at room temperature for 1 hour before serving. Adjust the seasonings before serving.

Mediterranean Chicken Orzo Salad

Serves 8 to 10

Juice of 1 1/2 lemons
3/4 cup olive oil
2 or 3 garlic cloves, minced
Salt and pepper to taste
2 cups orzo, cooked and drained
2 chicken breasts, roasted and chopped
24 kalamata olives, pitted
1 cup chopped drained oil-pack
    sun-dried tomatoes
8 ounces feta cheese, crumbled
1/2 cup pine nuts, toasted
1/2 bunch green onions, chopped
1/2 bunch fresh basil, chopped
1/2 bunch Italian parsley, chopped

Combine the lemon juice, olive oil, garlic, salt and pepper in a bowl and whisk to mix well. Combine the pasta, chicken, kalamata olives, sun-dried tomatoes, feta cheese, pine nuts, green onions, basil and parsley in a salad bowl and mix well. Add the dressing and toss to coat evenly.

Avocado Corn Salad

Serves 12

2 tablespoons olive oil
4 cups fresh corn kernels
1 teaspoon salt
3/4 teaspoon pepper
4 poblano chiles
1 large red bell pepper, chopped
4 scallions, thinly sliced diagonally
1/2 cup red wine vinegar
1/2 teaspoon fresh oregano
2 avocados, chopped

Heat the olive oil in a large skillet over medium heat. Add the corn, salt and pepper and sauté for 5 minutes. Spoon into a large bowl and let stand until cool.

Preheat the oven to 400 degrees. Place the poblano chiles in a roasting pan and roast for 10 minutes. Cool slightly. Remove the skins and seeds and chop the chiles.

Add the poblano chiles, bell pepper, scallions, wine vinegar and oregano to the corn; mix well. Let stand for 30 minutes or store in the refrigerator for up to 3 days. Add the avocado at serving time and mix gently. Serve at room temperature.

Italian Pasta Salad

Serves 10 to 12

Basil Dijon Vinaigrette
1/4 cup red wine vinegar
1/2 cup olive oil
1 garlic clove, minced
2 teaspoons Dijon mustard
1 teaspoon finely chopped basil
1/4 teaspoon salt
1/8 teaspoon pepper

Italian Pasta Salad
2 (9-ounce) packages cheese tortellini
3/4 cup salami strips
8 ounces mozzarella cheese,
    cut into cubes
1 (14-ounce) can artichoke hearts,
    drained and cut into quarters
1 or 2 tomatoes, cut into wedges
3/4 cup sliced red and/or yellow
    bell peppers
3 ounces black olives, sliced
2 tablespoons grated Parmesan cheese
1/4 cup chopped fresh Italian parsley
1 cup pine nuts (optional)

Vinaigrette
Combine the wine vinegar, olive oil, garlic, Dijon mustard, basil, salt and pepper in a bowl and whisk to mix well.

Salad
Cook the tortellini using the package directions; drain. Rinse with cold water and drain again; cool completely.

Combine the tortellini, salami, mozzarella cheese, artichoke hearts, tomato, bell peppers and black olives in a large bowl. Add the Parmesan cheese, parsley and pine nuts. Drizzle with the vinaigrette and toss to coat evenly. Chill until serving time.

Cheryl Forberg's Wild Rice Salad with Radicchio and Dried Cranberries

Serves 10

Forberg Vinaigrette
3 tablespoons balsamic vinegar
1/4 cup olive oil
1 tablespoon Dijon mustard
1/2 teaspoon salt
1/4 teaspoon freshly ground pepper

Wild Rice Salad with Radicchio and Dried Cranberries
1/2 cup dried cranberries
1/2 cup dry red wine
1 (12-ounce) head radicchio, cored and
    finely chopped
2 cups cooked wild rice
3 green onions, chopped with some
    green tops
3/4 cup chopped parsley
2 tablespoons slivered almonds,
    lightly toasted
Shaved Parmesan cheese (optional)

Vinaigrette
Combine the balsamic vinegar, olive oil, Dijon mustard, salt and pepper in a small bowl and whisk until smooth. Store in the refrigerator.

Salad
Combine the cranberries with the wine in a bowl. Let stand for 2 to 8 hours. Drain, discarding the wine or reserving it for another use.

Combine the cranberries with the radicchio, rice, green onions and parsley in a large bowl. Add the vinaigrette and toss gently. Sprinkle with the almonds and shaved Parmesan cheese. Serve at room temperature.

This recipe was adapted with permission from Positively Ageless: A 28-Day Plan for a Younger, Slimmer, Sexier You, *by Cheryl Forberg, RD (Rodale 2008). Cheryl Forberg, a registered dietician and professional chef, currently serves as nutritionist for the NBC reality series* The Biggest Loser *and as an advisor for* Prevention *magazine. She has written or contributed to nine books, including* Stop the Clock Cooking, The New Mayo Clinic Cookbook, *and* Healthy Heart Cookbook *for the American Medical Association. In 2005 she won the prestigious James Beard Award for healthy recipe development.*

Vanna White's Green Pea Salad

Serves 8

1¹/2 pounds fresh green peas
    in the shell
Salt to taste
6 slices bacon, crisp-cooked
    and crumbled
1 cup chopped celery
1 cup chopped pecans
1 cup chopped onion
¹/2 cup sour cream
¹/2 cup plain yogurt
Pepper to taste

Shell the green peas just before cooking. Combine with a small amount of lightly salted boiling water in a saucepan. Reduce the heat and simmer for 8 to 12 minutes or until done to taste; drain.

Combine the peas with the bacon, celery, pecans, onion, sour cream, yogurt, salt and pepper in a bowl and mix gently. Chill until serving time.

Since she made her debut on Wheel of Fortune, *Vanna White has built a phenomenal following worldwide. As America's favorite game show enters its twenty-sixth season in syndication, White has worn more than 5,100 different designer outfits at the puzzleboard, written a national bestselling autobiography, graced numerous magazine covers, and launched her own line of yarn. Beyond television, her favorite job is being a mom to her two children, Nicholas and Giovanna.*

Black Bean Soup

Serves 4

2 (15-ounce) cans black beans
2 (15-ounce) cans diced tomatoes
1/2 cup chopped red onion
1/2 cup chopped green bell pepper
2 jalapeño chiles, seeded and chopped
2 tablespoons chopped cilantro
     (optional)
1 garlic clove, minced
2 (15-ounce) cans chicken broth
3 tablespoons lime juice
2 tablespoons olive oil
1/2 teaspoon grated lime zest
Salt and pepper to taste

Combine the beans, tomatoes, onion, bell pepper, jalapeño chiles, cilantro and garlic in a large saucepan. Add the broth, lime juice, olive oil, lime zest, salt and pepper; mix well. Bring to a boil and cook for 5 minutes, stirring occasionally. Ladle into soup bowls and garnish with sour cream and shredded Cheddar cheese.

In 1833 Mexico took over the lands controlled by the missions and gave millions of acres as ranchos to Mexican citizens. California became a territory of the United States when the U.S. won the Mexican-American War in 1846. Gold was discovered at Sutter's Mill in 1848, and California became a state in 1850.

Gazpacho

Serves 6

4 cups chopped tomatoes

1 1/2 cups chopped green bell peppers

3/4 cup chopped onion

1 garlic clove, minced

2 cups beef bouillon

1/2 cup lemon juice

1/4 cup olive oil

Tabasco sauce to taste

1 tablespoon each paprika and salt

Freshly ground pepper to taste

1/2 cup sliced cucumber

Combine the tomatoes, bell peppers, onion and garlic in a large bowl. Add the beef bouillon, lemon juice, olive oil, Tabasco sauce, paprika, salt and pepper and mix well. Let stand at room temperature for 1 hour.

Chill in the refrigerator for 2 hours or longer. Add the cucumber just before serving and mix gently.

Roasted Tomato Basil Soup

Serves 6

3 pounds plum tomatoes, cut into halves

1/4 cup olive oil

1 teaspoon kosher salt

1 1/2 teaspoons crushed freshly
    ground pepper

2 cups chopped yellow onions

6 garlic cloves, minced

1/4 teaspoon crushed red pepper flakes

2 tablespoons unsalted butter

2 tablespoons olive oil

4 cups chicken stock or water

1 (28-ounce) can plum tomatoes

4 cups packed fresh basil leaves

1 teaspoon fresh thyme leaves

Preheat the oven to 400 degrees. Toss the tomato halves with 1/4 cup olive oil, the kosher salt and pepper in a bowl. Spread in a single layer in a baking pan. Roast for 45 minutes.

Sauté the onions, garlic and red pepper flakes in the butter and 2 tablespoons olive oil in an 8-quart stockpot for 10 minutes or until the onions begin to brown. Add the stock, undrained canned tomatoes, basil and thyme. Stir in the roasted tomatoes with any cooking juices.

Bring the mixture to a boil. Reduce the heat and simmer for 40 minutes. Process in a food processor fitted with the coarsest blade or in a food mill. Adjust the seasonings. Serve hot or chilled. Ladle into soup bowls and garnish with sour cream and/or fresh basil.

67

Ambrosia's Roasted Tomato, Saffron and Fennel Soup

Serves 6

6 tablespoons extra-virgin olive oil

12 garlic cloves

2 leek bulbs, sliced

1 Spanish onion, sliced

1 fennel bulb, sliced

1 rib celery, sliced

Pinch of chili flakes

1 cup white wine

Pinch of Spanish saffron

8 tomatoes, roasted and puréed

4 cups chicken stock

3 sprigs of fresh thyme

2 tablespoons chopped fresh basil

Juice of 1 lemon

1 tablespoon licorice liqueur

Kosher salt and freshly ground pepper
     to taste

Heat the olive oil in a 4-quart stockpot over medium heat. Add the garlic and sauté until light golden brown. Add the leeks, onion, fennel, celery and chili flakes. Sauté for 10 minutes or until the vegetables are tender, stirring occasionally with a wooden spoon.

Add the wine and saffron, stirring up the brown bits from the stockpot. Add the tomato purée, stock, thyme and basil. Bring to a simmer and cook for 20 to 25 minutes.

Purée the soup in a blender and strain through a fine mesh sieve. Season with the lemon juice, liqueur, kosher salt and pepper. Serve with warm toasted baguette to soak up every drop.

The OC Pavilion welcomes the return of a world-class dining experience at the five-star Ambrosia's Restaurant in Santa Ana. Executive Chef Michael Rossi has created a menu featuring "Seasonal Marketplace" cuisine that embraces California's most flavorful and fresh produce, fish, and livestock to create a dynamic balance between food and fine wines. A brick-domed, intimate wine cellar offers rare fine wines from around the world, and guests can experience tableside flambé desserts and live entertainment.

Tortilla Soup

Serves 6

1 tablespoon olive oil
3 (6- to 7-inch) corn tortillas
2 teaspoons olive oil
1 yellow onion, chopped
1 garlic clove, minced
1 (15-ounce) can tomatoes
2 (15-ounce) cans chicken broth
1/4 cup lime juice
Chili pepper to taste
1 avocado, chopped
2 cups shredded cooked chicken
1 cup (4 ounces) shredded
    Cheddar cheese
2 tablespoons chopped cilantro

Preheat the oven to 400 degrees. Spread 1 tablespoon olive oil in a baking pan. Cut the tortillas into halves and then into 1/2-inch strips. Arrange the strips in a single layer in the prepared pan. Bake until crisp.

Heat 2 teaspoons olive oil in a 3-quart saucepan over medium heat. Add the onion and garlic and sauté until the onion is tender. Drain the tomatoes, reserving the juice. Chop the tomatoes coarsely. Add the tomatoes, reserved tomato juice, broth, lime juice and chili pepper to the saucepan. Bring to a boil. Reduce the heat and simmer, covered, for 15 minutes.

Place the tortilla strips, avocado, chicken, Cheddar cheese and cilantro in separate bowls. Ladle the soup into bowls and allow guests to add the toppings of their choice.

The Golden Truffle's Tortilla Chicken Soup

Serves 4

4 cups homemade chicken stock
Salt and pepper to taste
8 corn tortillas, julienned
1 jalapeño chile, minced
1 shallot, minced
1 tablespoon olive oil
2 eggs, beaten
1 teaspoon chopped chipotle chile
1 bunch cilantro, chopped
1/2 cup crumbled Cotija cheese
1/2 cup sour cream

Bring the stock to a boil in a saucepan. Season with salt and pepper and keep warm.

Sauté the tortilla strips with the jalapeño chile and shallot in the olive oil in a skillet until the tortillas are softened. Add 1/2 cup of the stock, the eggs and chipotle chile and cook over medium heat until the eggs are soft-set and the tortillas are firm; do not overcook. Add the cilantro and mix well.

Scoop the egg mixture into the centers of four bowls and ladle the heated stock over the top. Sprinkle with the Cotija cheese and top with the sour cream.

The Golden Truffle began as a catering business and evolved into a restaurant that serves food with influences from France, Spain, the Caribbean, and Asia. Chef and owner Alan Greeley has taken the road less traveled, creating an Orange County favorite that satisfies customers of all tastes.

Hearty Sirloin Chili

Serves 8

2 pounds beef sirloin, cut into cubes
2 (10-ounce) cans diced tomatoes with
    green chiles
2 (16-ounce) cans tomato sauce
1 (6-ounce) can tomato paste
1 (7-ounce) can chopped green chiles
1 onion, chopped
2 teaspoons chili powder
1 teaspoon dried oregano leaves
1 teaspoon cayenne pepper
2 (30-ounce) cans black beans, drained
Salt and black pepper to taste
1 cup (4 ounces) shredded
    Cheddar cheese
1 bunch green onions, chopped

Combine the sirloin, tomatoes with green chiles, tomato sauce, tomato paste, green chiles and onion in a large stockpot. Add the chili powder, oregano and cayenne pepper and mix well. Bring to a boil. Reduce the heat and simmer, covered, for 2 hours.

Add the beans and simmer for 15 minutes. Season with salt and black pepper. Ladle into serving bowls. Sprinkle each serving with the Cheddar cheese and chopped green onions. Serve with a salad and freshly baked corn bread.

Black Bean Turkey Chili

Serves 8 to 10

2 tablespoons olive oil
2 cups chopped onions
1 red bell pepper, chopped
1 pound Italian-style turkey sausage,
    crumbled
2 pounds ground turkey
1 (12-ounce) can tomato paste
6 garlic cloves, minced
1 (8-ounce) can chopped green chiles
3 tablespoons chili powder
1 tablespoon dried oregano
1 tablespoon dried basil
1 teaspoon salt
1 teaspoon pepper
1 (30-ounce) can black beans, rinsed
    and drained
1 (28-ounce) can diced Italian-style
    plum tomatoes
1 (12-ounce) can beer
Tabasco sauce to taste
1/4 cup chopped fresh cilantro
    (optional)
Hot cooked rice

Heat the olive oil in a large skillet or saucepan over low heat. Add the onions and bell pepper and sauté for 10 minutes or until tender but not brown. Add the turkey sausage and ground turkey. Sauté over medium heat until cooked through and crumbly; drain.

Add the tomato paste, garlic, green chiles, chili powder, oregano, basil, salt and pepper; mix well. Stir in the beans, tomatoes, beer and Tabasco sauce. Bring to a simmer over low heat and simmer for 20 to 30 minutes. Adjust the seasonings and stir in the cilantro.

Serve over rice and garnish with sour cream, shredded Cheddar cheese, chopped onion and avocado.

Chicken Chili

Serves 6

4 chicken breasts
Salt and pepper to taste
2 tablespoons olive oil
2 (16-ounce) cans Great Northern beans,
    rinsed and drained
2 (10-ounce) cans tomatoes with
    green chiles
1 (16-ounce) can black beans, rinsed
    and drained
4 cups chicken broth
3 garlic cloves, crushed
2 teaspoons Worcestershire sauce
1 tablespoon brown sugar
1/2 envelope chili seasoning mix

Season the chicken with salt and pepper and cut into bite-size pieces. Sauté in the olive oil in a saucepan until no longer pink.

Combine 1 can of the beans and 1 can of the tomatoes with green chiles in a blender and purée. Add to the saucepan. Add the remaining beans and tomatoes with green chiles to the saucepan.

Add the black beans, broth, garlic, Worcestershire sauce, brown sugar and chili seasoning mix; mix well. Bring to a boil. Reduce the heat and simmer for 25 minutes. Ladle into serving bowls and garnish with sour cream and fresh parsley.

Note: For a vegetarian chili, omit the chicken and substitute vegetable stock for the chicken stock.

Chicken and White Bean Chili

Serves 8

4 cups chopped onions
2 garlic cloves, crushed
1 tablespoon olive oil
2 teaspoons ground cumin
1 teaspoon dried oregano, crushed
1/4 teaspoon ground cloves
1/4 teaspoon ground red pepper
4 (15-ounce) cans Great Northern beans,
    rinsed and drained
4 cups chicken broth
3 (4-ounce) cans chopped green chiles
4 cups chopped cooked chicken
2 cups (8 ounces) shredded Monterey
    Jack cheese
1 cup sour cream

Sauté the onions and garlic in the olive oil in a large stockpot until the onions are tender. Stir in the cumin, oregano, cloves and red pepper. Sauté for 2 to 3 minutes. Add the beans, broth and green chiles.

Bring the soup to a boil. Reduce the heat and simmer for 5 minutes. Add the chicken and simmer until heated through. Ladle into soup bowls and top each serving with the Monterey Jack cheese and sour cream.

Stir-Fried Asparagus

Serves 4

1 bunch asparagus
1 tablespoon olive oil
1 tablespoon Worcestershire sauce
2 tablespoons soy sauce
2 teaspoons ginger
2 tablespoons minced garlic
Pepper to taste
Pinch of sugar

Cut off and discard the stem ends of the asparagus. Slice the asparagus diagonally into 1/4-inch pieces. Heat the olive oil in a medium skillet over medium to high heat. Add the asparagus when you see bubbles form. Add the Worcestershire sauce, soy sauce, ginger, garlic, pepper and sugar one ingredient at a time, stir-frying until the asparagus is tender-crisp and coated with the seasonings. Serve with poultry or fish.

Grilled Asparagus with Sesame

Serves 4

1 bunch asparagus, trimmed
3 tablespoons sesame oil
Kosher salt to taste
Coarsely ground pepper to taste
2 tablespoons toasted sesame seeds

Preheat a grill on high heat. Combine the asparagus with the sesame oil, kosher salt and pepper in a sealable plastic bag and shake to coat evenly. Place the asparagus on the grill and grill for 4 to 5 minutes or until tender-crisp. Sprinkle with the sesame seeds and serve.

Baked Beans

Serves 8 to 12

8 ounces ground beef
8 ounces bacon, chopped
1 onion, chopped
1 (32-ounce) can pork and beans
1/3 cup packed brown sugar
1/3 cup granulated sugar
1/4 cup ketchup
1/4 cup barbecue sauce
1 tablespoon mustard
1/2 teaspoon chili powder

Preheat the oven to 350 degrees. Sauté the ground beef with the bacon and onion until the beef is brown and crumbly; drain. Add the pork and beans, brown sugar, granulated sugar, ketchup, barbecue sauce, mustard and chili powder; mix well. Spoon into a baking dish. Bake, uncovered, for 1 hour.

Note: The flavor improves if the beans are prepared the day before serving and reheated to serve.

Parmesan Green Beans

Serves 4

2 cups water
1 pound fresh green beans,
    trimmed
2 cups ice water
2 tablespoons olive oil
Salt and pepper to taste
2 tablespoons freshly grated
    Parmesan cheese

Bring 2 cups water to a boil in a saucepan. Add the green beans and cook for 8 minutes or until tender-crisp; drain. Plunge into the ice water to stop the cooking process and retain the color; drain. Pat dry on paper towels.

Combine with the olive oil, salt and pepper in a bowl and toss to coat evenly. Chill in the refrigerator for 8 hours or longer. Toss with the Parmesan cheese and serve.

Creamed Corn

Serves 8

2 (20-ounce) packages frozen
    corn kernels
1 cup heavy cream
1 cup milk
2 tablespoons sugar
1 teaspoon salt
Pinch of cayenne pepper
2 tablespoons butter, melted
2 tablespoons all-purpose flour
1/2 cup (2 ounces) grated
    Parmesan cheese

Preheat the broiler. Combine the corn with the heavy cream, milk, sugar, salt and cayenne pepper in a saucepan. Bring to a boil. Reduce the heat and simmer for 5 minutes. Blend the butter and flour together in a cup. Add to the corn mixture. Cook until thickened, stirring constantly.

Spoon into a baking dish and sprinkle with the Parmesan cheese. Broil for 3 to 5 minutes or until evenly brown.

Grilled Corn with Lime Butter and Tarragon

Serves 8

16 ears of corn, shucked
Olive oil
3/4 cup (11/2 sticks) butter
Juice of 2 limes
1/4 cup chopped tarragon
1 tablespoon pepper
Salt to taste

Preheat the grill. Brush the corn with olive oil. Grill until lightly charred on all sides. Cut the kernels from the cobs using a sharp knife and place in a bowl.

Melt the butter in a saucepan and cook until golden brown. Stir in the lime juice, tarragon, pepper and salt. Pour over the corn and mix well.

Potato and Leek Gratin

Serves 8 to 10

1 garlic clove
Butter for coating
3 pounds russet potatoes, peeled
    and very thinly sliced
2 large leek bulbs, thinly sliced
4 cups milk
3 garlic cloves, minced
1 fresh bay leaf
3 sprigs of fresh thyme
2 teaspoons salt
Salt and pepper to taste
Nutmeg to taste
1 to 2 cups (4 to 8 ounces) grated
    Gruyère cheese
2 tablespoons salted butter, chopped

Preheat the oven to 375 degrees. Rub a 9×12-inch baking dish with one garlic clove and coat with butter; discard the garlic clove.

Combine the potatoes with the leeks, milk, minced garlic, bay leaf, thyme and 2 teaspoons salt in a heavy saucepan. Bring to a boil. Reduce the heat and simmer until the potatoes are tender but still hold their shape. Drain, reserving the cooking liquid. Discard the bay leaf and thyme.

Layer half the potato mixture in the prepared dish. Sprinkle with salt, pepper, nutmeg and half the Gruyère cheese. Repeat the layers. Add enough of the reserved milk to reach the top of the layers. Dot with 2 tablespoons butter. Bake for 1 hour or until golden brown.

Roasted Potatoes

Serves 6 to 8

2¹/2 pounds small red potatoes or other
    color potatoes
3 tablespoons olive oil
2 tablespoons whole grain mustard
1¹/2 teaspoons kosher salt
1 teaspoon freshly ground pepper
¹/3 cup fresh Italian parsley, chopped
Kosher salt to taste

Preheat the oven to 425 degrees. Cut the potatoes into halves or quarters, depending on their size. Toss with the olive oil, mustard, 1¹/2 teaspoons kosher salt and the pepper in a bowl, coating well.

Spread on a baking sheet. Roast for 50 to 60 minutes or until light brown and tender, turning occasionally with a spatula to brown evenly.

Toss the potatoes with the parsley in a serving bowl and sprinkle with additional kosher salt.

Note: For variety, prepare this recipe with mixed colored small potatoes.

Garlic Rosemary Potatoes

Serves 4

2 pounds small red potatoes,
    cut into chunks
1/4 cup olive oil
5 garlic cloves, crushed
1 1/2 tablespoons fresh rosemary
1 teaspoon grated lemon zest
Coarse salt and freshly ground pepper
    to taste

Place an oven rack in the lower third of the oven. Preheat the oven to 450 degrees. Line a baking pan with foil.

Combine the potatoes with the olive oil, garlic, rosemary and lemon zest in a large bowl; mix to coat evenly. Spread in the prepared pan.

Roast for 20 minutes. Turn the potatoes with a spatula and roast for 10 minutes longer or until crisp and golden brown. Season with coarse salt and pepper.

In 1913 the first avocado grove was planted by John T. Wheedon in the city of Yorba Linda.

Spanakopita

Serves 6 to 8

2 tablespoons olive oil
1 onion, chopped
2 pounds fresh spinach
4 eggs, beaten
16 ounces cream cheese, chopped
8 ounces mozzarella cheese, shredded
8 ounces Cheddar cheese, shredded
8 to 12 ounces feta cheese, crumbled
1 garlic clove, minced
2 teaspoons dried mint leaves
Salt and pepper to taste
1 pound frozen phyllo dough, thawed
2 cups (4 sticks) butter, melted

Heat 1 tablespoon of the olive oil in a skillet over medium heat. Add half the onion and sauté for 1 minute. Add half the spinach and press down. Turn the spinach over to coat both sides. Cook, covered, over low heat for 2 minutes, stirring occasionally. Remove to a bowl; the spinach may not be completely wilted. Repeat the process with the remaining olive oil, onion and spinach.

Combine the spinach mixture in a bowl and add the eggs, cream cheese, mozzarella cheese, Cheddar cheese, feta cheese, garlic, mint, salt and pepper; mix well.

Line a 9×13-inch baking pan with six to eight sheets of the phyllo dough, brushing each sheet with the butter. Spread with half the spinach mixture. Add three sheets of phyllo dough, brushing each sheet with the butter. Spread with the remaining spinach mixture and top with the remaining phyllo dough, brushing each sheet with the butter.

Tuck in the edges of the dough with a knife. Score the top into squares with a knife, cutting halfway into the layers. Chill in the refrigerator for 10 to 15 minutes.

Preheat the oven to 350 degrees. Bake the spanakopita for 50 to 60 minutes or until the phyllo is medium dark golden brown; watch the edges and bottom to prevent burning. Let stand to cool for 20 to 30 minutes. Cut though the scored marks to serve.

Note: Cover opened phyllo dough with a damp cloth until needed.

Maple Bacon Acorn Squash

Serves 6

3 acorn squash, about 1 1/2 pounds
2 slices bacon
2 tablespoons maple syrup or honey
1 tablespoon balsamic vinaigrette

Cut the squash into halves lengthwise and discard the seeds. Place cut side up in a microwave-safe dish. Cover with plastic wrap, turning one corner back to vent. Microwave on High for 12 to 14 minutes or until tender.

Fry the bacon in a skillet for 8 to 10 minutes or until crisp, turning occasionally; drain.

Blend the syrup and vinaigrette in a small bowl. Place the squash on serving plates. Brush the cut surfaces of the squash with the syrup mixture. Crumble the bacon over the squash and serve.

Calabacitas

Serves 8

2 1/2 cups chopped yellow
    summer squash
2 1/2 cups chopped zucchini
1 cup fresh or frozen corn
1 cup chopped Roma tomatoes
1 red onion, chopped
3 jalapeño chiles, seeded and chopped
3 garlic cloves, minced
1/2 cup fresh cilantro, chopped
2 tablespoons butter, melted
2 tablespoons olive oil
Salt and freshly ground pepper to taste

Preheat the oven to 375 degrees. Combine the squash, zucchini, corn, tomatoes, onion, jalapeño chiles, garlic and cilantro in a bowl. Add the butter, olive oil, salt and pepper and toss to mix well. Spread in a baking dish. Bake for 25 to 35 minutes or until the vegetables are tender, stirring several times.

Note: For variety, add 1/2 cup heavy cream and/or 1 cup shredded Monterey Jack cheese or Cheddar cheese during the last 10 minutes of baking time. For a complete meal, add cooked ground beef or chopped cooked chicken.

Jasmine Rice with Garlic, Ginger and Cilantro

Serves 6 to 8

3 cups jasmine rice
3 tablespoons canola oil
1/3 cup finely chopped gingerroot
3 garlic cloves, minced
3 1/2 cups low-sodium chicken broth
1 cup coconut milk
Salt to taste
3/4 teaspoon chopped fresh cilantro

Rinse the rice in a large sieve under cold water until the water runs clear; drain. Heat the canola oil in a large heavy saucepan over medium-high heat. Add the gingerroot and garlic and sauté for 30 seconds or until fragrant. Add the rice and sauté for 3 minutes.

Stir in the broth, coconut milk and salt. Add the cilantro and mix well. Bring to a boil; reduce the heat to medium-low. Cook, covered, for 15 minutes or until the rice is tender. Remove from the heat and let stand, covered, for 10 minutes. Fluff the rice with a fork and serve immediately.

Fried Rice

Serves 4 to 6

1 tablespoon olive oil
2 eggs, beaten
1 onion, cut into halves and sliced
1 garlic clove, minced
2 tablespoons olive oil
4 ounces uncooked shrimp, chopped
1/2 cup chopped cooked ham, chicken
    or pork
1/2 cup julienned carrots
1/2 cup frozen peas
2 cups cooked rice, chilled
1 to 3 tablespoons soy sauce
Salt and pepper to taste
4 scallions, chopped

Heat 1 tablespoon olive oil in a skillet over low heat. Add the eggs and cook until soft-set. Remove to a bowl. Stir-fry the onion and garlic in 2 tablespoons olive oil in the skillet until golden brown.

Add the shrimp and stir-fry for 1 minute. Add the ham, carrots and peas and stir-fry until heated through. Stir in the eggs, rice, soy sauce, salt and pepper. Stir-fry until heated through. Stir in the scallions and serve hot.

Dawn Patrol

Entrées

Dawn Patrol—*noun*—a surfer who arrives at the beach at or just before sunrise. The dawn patrol is a special breed of surfers who, armed with the knowledge of weather patterns and predicted swells, make it their mission to start each day in solitude looking to be the first to ride the waves that have come up overnight. A drive up and down the coast will unveil members of the dawn patrol looking for that perfect wave to start their day. After the dawn patrollers head off to work or school or back to bed, the forty-two miles of beach in Orange County become a playground for Southern Californians.

Huntington Beach is the epitome of beach life in The OC. Famously known as Surf City USA®, Huntington Beach is home to the US Open of Surfing, AVP Pro Beach Volleyball, and the Surf City USA® Marathon. Newport Beach is California's premier oceanside retreat with intimate sandy beaches, a jetty called "The Wedge" where body surfers flock, and the historic Balboa Pavilion built in 1905. Laguna Beach boasts the best tide pools and scuba diving in the area. Dana Point, dubbed "the only romantic cove in California" by founder Richard Henry Dana, was the only major harbor between San Diego and Santa Barbara at the turn of the nineteenth century. Dana Point is now home to the Orange County Ocean Institute and is a popular spot for whale watching.

The beach is at the heart of Orange County's love affair with the outdoors and the biggest part of who we are. From Seal Beach in North Orange County to San Onofre in the South, the beach cities draw visitors from all over the country.

Zov's Bistro's Beef Tenderloin with Shallot Thyme Sauce

Serves 6 to 8

Beef Tenderloin

1 (2$^{1}/_{2}$- to 3-pound) beef
 tenderloin, trimmed
2 tablespoons olive oil
2 tablespoons minced garlic
1$^{1}/_{2}$ tablespoons coarsely chopped
 fresh rosemary
1 teaspoon salt
1 teaspoon coarsely ground pepper
1 tablespoon olive oil
2 tablespoons Dijon mustard
1 tablespoon olive oil

Shallot Thyme Sauce

1 tablespoon butter
1 tablespoon minced garlic
1 tablespoon minced shallot
1 tablespoon chopped fresh thyme
1$^{3}/_{4}$ cups beef stock or beef broth
$^{1}/_{4}$ cup ($^{1}/_{2}$ stick) unsalted butter,
 chopped and chilled
Coarsely ground pepper to taste

Tenderloin

Tie the tenderloin with kitchen twine to hold its shape; place in a heavy baking pan. Combine 2 tablespoons olive oil with the garlic, rosemary, salt and pepper in a small bowl and mix well. Rub all but 1 tablespoon of the garlic mixture over the beef. Add 1 tablespoon olive oil and the Dijon mustard to the garlic mixture. Cover the tenderloin and the mustard mixture separately and chill in the refrigerator for 2 to 12 hours.

Preheat the oven to 400 degrees. Heat 1 tablespoon olive oil in a large nonstick skillet over high heat. Add the tenderloin and sear for 5 minutes or until brown on all sides. Return to the baking pan and set the skillet aside to use for the sauce. Spread the mustard mixture over the tenderloin. Roast for 30 minutes for medium-rare, 130 degrees on a meat thermometer, or until done to taste. Remove from the oven and tent with foil to keep warm.

Sauce

Discard the oil and any brown bits in the skillet. Melt 1 tablespoon butter in the skillet over medium heat. Add the garlic and shallot and sauté for 1 minute. Stir in the thyme and stock. Bring to a simmer over high heat. Reduce the heat and simmer for 8 minutes or until reduced by half, stirring frequently. Remove from the heat and whisk in the chopped butter one piece at a time, stirring until melted and smooth after each addition. Season with pepper.

**Beef Tenderloin with
Shallot Thyme Sauce** continued

Assembly

Cut the tenderloin crosswise into $1/2$-inch slices. Arrange on serving plates or a platter and drizzle with the sauce. Serve immediately with roasted asparagus, potato gratin or mashed potatoes. For a colorful, low-fat meal, serve the tenderloin on a bed of braised spinach with a side of teardrop tomatoes tossed in olive oil and basil.

Note: This roast beef tenderloin makes a stunning entrée for a special occasion. Tenderloin is a lean and elegant cut of beef, but it has a bold enough flavor to handle the big flavors of coarsely ground pepper and spicy mustard. Buy the best quality beef you can find for this recipe. If you are hosting a party, make this dish a day in advance so you will have more time to mingle with your guests. Sear the beef, spread it with the mustard mixture and store in the refrigerator until time to roast it.

Pomegranate sauce is a great alternative to the peppery sauce suggested here; its zippy flavor enhances the beef. Cut any leftover beef into thin slices and serve in sandwiches with thick slices of avocado and tomatoes on whole grain bread, or serve atop a summer salad drizzled with balsamic vinaigrette.

Zov's Bistro, Bakery & Neighborhood Cafes serve the finest Mediterranean cuisine in a chic, yet comfortable, environment. Founded in 1987 by Zov Karamardian, Zov's Bistro in Tustin has become one of the most recognized restaurants in Orange County. In 2007 Zov's Neighborhood Cafes were launched in Newport Coast and Irvine, establishing Zov's culinary empire and tradition. All three locations offer brunch, lunch, and dinner dining as well as special events catering.

Grilled Flank Steak with Sour Orange and Garlic Mojo

Serves 4

Sour Orange and Garlic Mojo

10 garlic cloves

2 habanero chiles or other spicy chiles,
    seeded and minced

4 teaspoons cumin seeds, toasted

1 teaspoon salt

1 cup olive oil

1/3 cup orange juice

1/3 cup lime juice

1 1/2 tablespoons sherry vinegar

Salt and freshly cracked pepper to taste

Grilled Flank Steak

1 (1 1/2-pound) flank steak

Salt and freshly cracked pepper to taste

2 large red onions, thickly sliced

Olive oil

Mojo

Combine the garlic, habanero chiles, cumin seeds and 1 teaspoon salt in a food processor and pulse until finely chopped but not puréed. Remove to a bowl. Heat the olive oil in a sauté pan until hot but not smoking. Pour over the chile mixture and stir to mix well and partially cook the garlic. Let stand for 10 minutes.

Whisk the orange juice and lime juice in a cup. Whisk into the garlic mixture with the vinegar. Season with salt and pepper and cool completely.

Steak

Place the steak in a shallow dish and coat with 1 cup of the cooled mojo, reserving the remaining mojo. Marinate for 1 to 4 hours.

Preheat a grill. Remove the steak from the marinade and pat dry; discard the marinade. Season with salt and pepper. Grill the steak on one side for 6 minutes. Turn and grill for 4 minutes longer or until medium-rare. Remove to a cutting board. Brush the onions with olive oil and grill until tender.

Warm the reserved mojo in a saucepan. Slice the steak crosswise diagonally and serve with the grilled onions and warmed mojo.

Stuffed Flank Steak

Serves 6

1 (2-pound) flank steak
Salt and pepper to taste
8 ounces prosciutto, sliced
8 ounces mozzarella cheese, sliced
1 pound turkey sausage
$1/2$ cup chopped fresh parsley, or
    $1/4$ cup parsley flakes
$1/4$ cup chopped green onions
3 garlic cloves, minced
1 egg, beaten
2 tablespoons dried Italian herbs
1 teaspoon cayenne pepper
6 tablespoons olive tapenade
$1/4$ cup olive oil

Preheat the oven to 375 degrees. Pound the steak $1/4$-inch thick with a meat mallet. Season with salt and pepper on both sides. Layer the prosciutto slices and mozzarella slices evenly over the steak, covering completely.

Remove the turkey sausage from the casings and crumble into a bowl. Add the parsley, green onions, garlic, egg, Italian herbs and cayenne pepper and mix well. Spread over the prepared steak. Top with the olive tapenade.

Roll the steak from the long side to enclose the filling; tie at 1-inch intervals to secure. Heat the olive oil in a large skillet over medium heat. Add the steak and sear on all sides. Remove to a baking pan. Bake for 30 minutes.

Orange Braised Beef

Serves 4 to 6

1 orange
2¹/2 pounds boneless beef short ribs
    or stew meat
Salt and freshly ground pepper to taste
1 tablespoon olive oil
¹/2 large yellow onion, chopped
2 carrots, chopped
1 rib celery, chopped
1 teaspoon minced garlic
1 cup red wine
1 bay leaf
1 cup (or more) beef broth or
    chicken broth
1 pound red new potatoes,
    cut into halves

Remove just the orange portion of half the orange peel in strips with a peeler, taking care not to include any of the bitter white pith. Reserve the orange for another use.

Season the beef with salt and pepper. Heat the olive oil in a large saucepan over medium heat. Add the beef in batches, searing on all sides; remove to a bowl. Drain the excess drippings from the saucepan, leaving the brown bits in the bottom.

Sauté the onion, carrots and celery in the saucepan until nearly tender. Add the garlic and sauté until the vegetables are tender. Add the wine and simmer until reduced by half. Stir in the bay leaf and orange peel.

Return the beef to the saucepan and add enough beef broth to almost cover the beef and vegetables. Simmer, covered, for 1¹/2 hours or until tender, stirring occasionally and adding additional broth as needed.

Add the potatoes and cook for 30 to 40 minutes longer or until the potatoes are fork-tender. Discard the bay leaf and any orange peel that did not cook into the sauce. Simmer, uncovered, until the sauce is reduced to the desired consistency. Adjust the seasonings and serve with polenta, rice or crusty bread.

Bolognese Sauce

Serves 6

1 tablespoon butter
1 tablespoon olive oil
2 carrots
2 ribs celery
1 sweet onion
2 pounds ground round
Garlic salt, salt and pepper to taste
1 (28-ounce) can crushed tomatoes
1 (6-ounce) can tomato paste
3 tablespoons light brown sugar
1 cup heavy cream
Hot cooked pasta

Melt the butter with the olive oil in a medium saucepan. Process the carrots in a food processor until chopped. Add the celery and then the onion, processing until chopped. Add the chopped vegetables to the saucepan and cook over very low heat for 15 to 20 minutes, stirring frequently.

Season the ground beef with garlic salt, salt and pepper. Sauté in a skillet until brown and crumbly. Add to the vegetable mixture.

Stir in the tomatoes gradually. Adjust the seasonings and bring to a simmer. Stir in the tomato paste and adjust the seasonings again. Bring to a simmer and stir in the brown sugar. Add the cream and cook over low heat for 30 to 45 minutes until thickened to the desired consistency.

Serve over pasta and garnish with freshly grated Parmesan cheese. The sauce can be reheated over low heat.

Hide-the-Veggies Meat Loaf

Serves 6

1 pound lean ground beef
1 pound lean ground turkey
1 small onion, chopped
1 green bell pepper, chopped
1 large zucchini, shredded
1 carrot, shredded
1 (10-ounce) package frozen chopped
    spinach, thawed and squeezed dry
1¹/₂ cups oats
2 eggs, beaten
¹/₂ cup (2 ounces) grated
    Parmesan cheese
2 garlic cloves, minced
1 tablespoon Worcestershire sauce
1 tablespoon hot sauce
2 tablespoons dried basil
1 tablespoon parsley flakes
1¹/₂ teaspoons kosher salt
1 teaspoon freshly ground pepper
1 cup tomato sauce
1 small onion, sliced into rings
Salt and pepper to taste

Preheat the oven to 375 degrees. Combine the ground beef, ground turkey, chopped onion, bell pepper, zucchini, carrot and spinach in a bowl. Add the oats, eggs, Parmesan cheese, garlic, Worcestershire sauce, hot sauce, basil, parsley, 1¹/₂ teaspoons kosher salt and 1 teaspoon pepper; mix well.

Press into an oiled loaf pan or shape into a loaf in an oiled baking dish. Spread the tomato sauce evenly over the loaf and arrange the onion rings over the top. Sprinkle with additional salt and pepper. Bake for 50 to 60 minutes or to 160 degrees on a meat thermometer. Let stand at room temperature for 5 minutes. Slice to serve.

Ruby's Aegean Burger

Serves 1

1 beef hamburger patty
2 ounces feta cheese
2 ounces grilled onion
1 hamburger bun
1 1/2 tablespoons margarine
1 1/2 tablespoons mayonnaise
1/2 teaspoon oregano
1 lettuce leaf
1 slice tomato

Preheat the grill to 350 degrees. Grill the hamburger patty until done to taste. Place the feta cheese in a microwave-safe dish and microwave for 15 seconds to soften. Place on the hamburger patty and grill for 30 seconds to melt the cheese slightly. Top with the grilled onion.

Spread the cut sides of the bun with margarine and grill until golden brown. Remove the bottom bun portion from the grill and spread with the mayonnaise. Sprinkle with the oregano and top with the lettuce and tomato. Cover the grilled hamburger patty with the top bun portion and place on the bottom. Serve with a pickle spear.

The bright red vinyl booths, white Formica tables, and soda fountains at Ruby's Diner have made this family-friendly establishment a southern California favorite. Enjoy the 1940s nostalgic atmosphere while dining on a variety of Ruby favorites like the Hickory Burger, American Kobe Chopped Steak, Chili Fries, Clam Chowder, and much more. And don't forget a deluxe malt or shake! Landmark Pier locations include Balboa, Huntington Beach, Seal Beach, and Oceanside.

Veal with Creamy Tarragon Sauce

Serves 4

2 tablespoons all-purpose flour
Pinch of nutmeg
Salt and freshly ground pepper to taste
3 pounds veal, cut into bite-size pieces
2 tablespoons butter
2 tablespoons olive oil
1/4 cup shredded carrots
2 shallots, chopped
2 sprigs of fresh tarragon, chopped
3/4 cup dry white wine
2 tablespoons water
3/4 cup heavy cream
Hot cooked rice
1/4 cup fresh parsley, chopped

Mix the flour, nutmeg, salt and pepper in a bowl. Add the veal and toss to coat evenly. Melt the butter with the olive oil in a large skillet. Add the veal and sauté until brown on all sides. Sprinkle with the carrots, shallots and tarragon.

Add the wine and water. Bring to a boil. Reduce the heat and simmer for 25 minutes. Stir in the cream and cook until thickened, stirring frequently. Serve over rice and sprinkle with the parsley.

Tangy Pork Roast in the Slow Cooker

Serves 4

1 large onion, sliced
1 (1 1/2-pound) boneless pork loin roast
1 cup hot water
1/4 cup sugar
3 tablespoons red wine vinegar
2 tablespoons soy sauce
1 tablespoon ketchup
Dash of hot pepper sauce
1/4 teaspoon garlic powder
1/2 teaspoon each salt and pepper

Arrange the onion over the bottom of the slow cooker and place the roast on the onions. Combine the hot water, sugar, wine vinegar, soy sauce, ketchup, hot sauce, garlic powder, salt and pepper in a bowl and mix well. Pour over the roast. Cook on Low for 5 to 7 hours, on High for 2 to 3 hours or to 170 degrees on a meat thermometer.

Pork Tenderloin with Figs

Serves 6

2 pork tenderloins
6 ounces gorgonzola cheese or other
    blue cheese, thinly sliced
6 dried figs, sliced
Splash of white wine

Preheat the oven to 350 degrees. Slice the tenderloins lengthwise, cutting to but not through the opposite side. Spread the tenderloins open on a work surface. Arrange the blue cheese down the centers of the tenderloins and top with the sliced figs. Close the two sides of the tenderloins to enclose the filling and tie at 2-inch intervals with kitchen twine or fasten with wooden picks to secure.

Place in a baking dish and drizzle with wine. Roast for 30 to 35 minutes or to the desired degree of doneness. Remove from the oven and let stand for several minutes. Slice to serve.

Note: For variety, substitute sun-dried tomatoes and boursin cheese, spinach and feta cheese, or chives and pesto for the blue cheese and figs. You can also add apple jelly or orange marmalade as a glaze instead of white wine.

Cathy Thomas's Pork Chops with Pomegranate Relish

Serves 4

Pomegranate Relish

2 small fennel bulbs
2 tablespoons olive oil or vegetable oil
1/4 cup finely chopped red onion
2 teaspoons honey
1 teaspoon seasoned rice vinegar
1/2 teaspoon cider vinegar
1 cup pomegranate seeds
2 tablespoons chopped fresh cilantro
2 tablespoons chopped fresh parsley
Salt and freshly ground pepper to taste

Pork Chops

4 (1/2- to 3/4-inch-thick) pork chops,
     patted dry
Salt and pepper to taste
1 tablespoon olive oil or vegetable oil

Relish

Trim the fennel bulbs and cut into halves, removing the cores and reserving the fronds. Cut the bulbs into 1/4-inch pieces. Heat the olive oil in a medium skillet over high heat. Add the fennel and toss to coat evenly. Reduce the heat to medium and sauté for 10 minutes or until tender. Add the onion and sauté for 1 to 2 minutes or until nearly tender. Remove to a medium bowl.

Stir in the honey, rice vinegar and cider vinegar. Add the pomegranate seeds, cilantro, parsley, salt and pepper; mix gently.

Pork Chops

Season the pork chops with salt and pepper. Heat the olive oil in a large skillet over medium-high heat until hot. Add the pork chops and cook for 4 to 5 minutes on each side or until brown and cooked through. Serve topped with the relish. Garnish with the reserved fennel fronds.

California Chicken

Serves 4

4 chicken breasts
Salt and pepper to taste
2 large tomatoes, cut into wedges
1/2 cup chopped onion
6 large brown mushrooms, sliced
1/2 cup California olives, sliced
1/2 cup dry cooking sherry
1 1/2 tablespoons fresh lemon juice
1/2 teaspoon dried basil
1/2 teaspoon dried marjoram
1 teaspoon celery salt
1 avocado, sliced
4 slices medium Cheddar cheese
Hot cooked rice pilaf

Preheat the oven to 350 degrees. Place each chicken breast on a 12×18-inch piece of baking parchment or foil. Sprinkle with salt and pepper. Top evenly with the tomatoes, onion, mushrooms and olives.

Combine the sherry, lemon juice, basil, marjoram and celery salt in a cup and mix well. Drizzle evenly over the chicken. Fold and seal the baking parchment to make four individual packets. Place in a baking pan. Bake for 45 minutes without turning.

Open the packets carefully to avoid the hot steam; top with the avocado and cheese. Refold the baking parchment and let stand for 2 minutes to melt the cheese. Serve over rice pilaf.

Note: The packets will be very juicy. Pierce the baking parchment or foil with a fork before unwrapping and allow the juices to drizzle over the rice pilaf. For a lower-fat version, omit the cheese and avocado.

Grilled Lemon Chicken

Serves 6

3/4 cup fresh lemon juice
1/2 cup extra-virgin olive oil
1/2 teaspoon dried thyme, or
    1 tablespoon chopped fresh thyme
2 teaspoons kosher salt
1 teaspoon freshly ground pepper
2 pounds boneless skinless
    chicken breasts

Combine the lemon juice, olive oil, thyme, kosher salt and pepper in a small bowl; whisk to mix well. Pour over the chicken in a nonreactive bowl with a lid or a sealable plastic bag. Marinate in the refrigerator for 6 to 12 hours or freeze until needed.

Preheat a charcoal grill. Drain the chicken and place on the grill. Grill for 10 minutes on each side or until cooked through. Cool slightly and cut diagonally into 1/2-inch slices.

Grilled Chili Lime Chicken with Strawberry Salsa

Serves 4

Grilled Chili Lime Chicken
2 tablespoons lime juice
1 tablespoon grapeseed oil or other
    mild-flavored vegetable oil
1 tablespoon acacia honey, clover honey
    or other mild-flavored honey
2 garlic cloves, minced
1 teaspoon chili powder
4 (4-ounce) boneless skinless
    chicken breasts

Strawberry Salsa
8 large strawberries, chopped
1/3 cup finely chopped white onion
1 tablespoon finely chopped
    fresh cilantro
1 tablespoon lime juice
1/4 teaspoon chili powder
Salt and freshly ground pepper to taste

Chicken
Combine the lime juice, grapeseed oil, honey, garlic and chili powder in a medium bowl and whisk until smooth. Combine with the chicken in a large sealable plastic bag. Place in a shallow bowl and marinate on the bottom shelf of the refrigerator for 4 to 12 hours, turning the bag occasionally.

Preheat the grill to medium-high heat. Drain the chicken and place on the grill. Grill for 12 minutes or to 170 degrees on a meat thermometer, turning once. Remove to a platter and let stand for 5 minutes before slicing to serve.

Salsa
Combine the strawberries, onion, cilantro, lime juice and chili powder in a small bowl. Season with salt and pepper. Serve with the chicken.

Chicken Breasts Stuffed with Spinach and Camembert Cheese

Serves 4

1 tablespoon olive oil
16 ounces fresh baby spinach
1 garlic clove, minced
$1/8$ teaspoon freshly grated nutmeg
Salt and freshly ground pepper to taste
4 ounces chilled Camembert cheese or
    $1/2$ cup crumbled feta cheese
4 (6-ounce) boneless skinless
    chicken breasts
$1/3$ cup all-purpose flour
$1/4$ teaspoon salt
$1/8$ teaspoon pepper
1 tablespoon olive oil
$3/4$ cup dry white wine
1 tablespoon margarine

Heat 1 tablespoon olive oil in a skillet over medium-high heat. Add the spinach gradually, sautéing each addition until wilted before adding more. Add the garlic and cook for 1 minute or until all the spinach is wilted. Remove to a colander and press out as much liquid as possible; set the skillet aside for the chicken.

Chop the spinach on a cutting board; combine with the nutmeg and salt and pepper to taste in a bowl. Remove the rind from the Camembert cheese and finely chop the cheese. Add to the spinach mixture and mix well.

Cut a horizontal pocket in each chicken breast, taking care not to cut all the way through. Spoon one-fourth of the spinach mixture into each pocket and secure the edges with wooden picks.

Mix the flour with $1/2$ teaspoon salt and $1/8$ teaspoon pepper. Coat the chicken with the flour mixture, shaking off any excess. Wipe out the skillet with a paper towel. Heat 1 tablespoon olive oil in the skillet over medium-high heat. Add the chicken and sauté for 6 to 8 minutes or until light brown on both sides, turning once. Add the wine and reduce the heat to medium-low. Cook for 10 minutes or until the chicken is cooked through, turning once.

Remove the chicken to a platter. Cook the liquid in the skillet for 2 to 3 minutes or until reduced to $1/3$ cup. Whisk in the margarine. Pour over the chicken and serve immediately.

Orange Herbed Chicken

Serves 8

8 bone-in chicken breasts with skin
Salt and pepper to taste
2 tablespoons butter
2 tablespoons olive oil
1 1/2 cups chicken broth
3/4 cup fresh orange juice
1/2 teaspoon grated orange zest
2 sprigs of tarragon
2 sprigs of thyme
1/4 cup (1/2 stick) butter, sliced
1/2 cup slivered almonds

Preheat the oven to 375 degrees. Season the chicken with salt and pepper. Heat 2 tablespoons butter with the olive oil in a large skillet over high heat for 2 minutes. Add the chicken skin side down and sear for 1 minute or until the skin is crisp and golden brown. Turn the chicken and sear for 1 minute longer. Remove to a baking dish. Bake for 30 to 40 minutes or until the juices run clear.

Add the broth, orange juice, orange zest, tarragon and thyme to the skillet. Cook until the mixture is reduced by about three-fourths and coats the back of the spoon, stirring frequently. Whisk in 1/4 cup butter until smooth just before serving. Season with salt and pepper.

Place the chicken on serving plates and spoon the sauce over the top; sprinkle with the almonds.

Parmesan-Crusted Chicken with Sage Butter Sauce

Serves 4

Parmesan-Crusted Chicken

4 boneless skinless chicken breasts,
    at room temperature
1/2 cup all-purpose flour
Salt and freshly ground pepper to taste
1 egg
Juice of 1 lemon
3/4 cup dry bread crumbs
1/2 cup (2 ounces) grated
    Parmesan cheese
1 tablespoon chopped fresh parsley
1 tablespoon chopped fresh sage
Grated zest of 1 lemon
1 teaspoon kosher salt
1/4 teaspoon freshly ground pepper
3 tablespoons olive oil

Sage Butter Sauce

2 shallots, minced
1 garlic clove, minced
2 tablespoons butter
1/2 cup dry white wine
1/2 cup heavy cream
1/2 cup chicken broth
Juice and grated zest of 1 lemon
2 tablespoon butter, chopped
2 tablespoons chopped fresh sage
Salt, freshly ground black pepper and
    cayenne pepper to taste

Chicken

Preheat the oven to 450 degrees. Place each chicken breast in a plastic bag and add a small amount of water. Pound each to an even thickness.

Combine the flour with salt and pepper. Whisk the egg with the lemon juice in a shallow dish. Mix the bread crumbs, Parmesan cheese, parsley, sage, lemon zest, 1 teaspoon kosher salt and 1/4 teaspoon pepper in a shallow dish. Coat the chicken with the flour mixture. Dip into the egg mixture and coat with the bread crumb mixture, pressing the crumbs over both sides of the chicken.

Heat the olive oil in a large skillet. Add the chicken and sauté for 3 minutes or until golden brown on the bottom. Turn the chicken and sauté for 2 to 3 minutes longer. Remove to a lightly oiled baking dish. Roast for 8 to 10 minutes or until cooked through. Slice the chicken to serve.

Sauce

Sauté the shallots and garlic in 2 tablespoons butter in a small saucepan until tender. Add the wine, cream, broth, lemon juice and lemon zest. Simmer for 10 minutes or until reduced by half. Whisk in 2 tablespoons butter 1/2 tablespoon at a time. Add the sage and mix well. Season with salt, black pepper and cayenne pepper. Keep warm until serving time.

Serve the sauce over the sliced chicken. Serve with Garlic Rosemary Potatoes (page 80).

Note: To make the bread crumbs, select a day-old loaf of rustic bread with a chewy texture like ciabatta rather than a hard-crusted bread. Cut the loaf into 1-inch pieces and process into crumbs in a food processor. Freeze any unused crumbs in a sealable plastic bag.

Prosciutto Chicken Cutlets

Serves 4

4 boneless skinless chicken breasts
3 tablespoons butter
1 teaspoon oregano
1/4 teaspoon freshly ground pepper
4 very thin slices prosciutto
4 slices mozzarella cheese
1/4 cup dry white wine

Pound the chicken to a thickness of 1/4-inch. Melt the butter in a large skillet over medium heat. Add the chicken and sauté for 3 minutes on each side. Season with the oregano and pepper. Place one slice of prosciutto and one slice of cheese on each piece of chicken. Drizzle with the wine. Cover the skillet and cook for 5 minutes or until the cheese melts and the chicken is cooked through.

Tex-Mex Chicken

Serves 8

Juice of 1 lemon
4 garlic cloves, minced
3 tablespoons coarse sea salt
3 tablespoons sweet Hungarian paprika
1 to 2 tablespoons cayenne pepper
8 bone-in chicken breasts with skin, or
　　other chicken pieces

Mix the lemon juice and garlic together. Mix the sea salt, paprika and cayenne pepper together. Rub the chicken on both sides with the garlic mixture and sprinkle with the paprika mixture. Place skin side up in a baking dish and marinate, covered, in the refrigerator for 8 to 12 hours.

Preheat the oven to 300 degrees. Roast the chicken for 1 hour. Remove to a heated grill and grill for 8 to 10 minutes on each side.

Chicken Chilaquiles

Serves 8 to 10

4 bone-in chicken breasts with skin
Salt and pepper to taste
2 cups chicken stock
1 sweet onion, very thinly sliced
3 1/2 cups fresh tomato salsa
1/2 cup heavy cream
1 teaspoon salt
1/2 teaspoon pepper
1/2 cup vegetable oil
12 corn tortillas
1 cup (4 ounces) shredded
    manchego cheese
1 cup crumbled Cotija cheese
1 cup crumbled queso fresco

Season the chicken with salt and pepper. Bring the stock to a boil in a large saucepan over high heat. Add the chicken and reduce the heat to medium. Cook, covered, for 15 minutes. Let stand in the stock until cool. Shred the chicken into bite-size pieces, discarding the skin and bones; reserve the stock for another use. Combine the chicken with the onion in a large bowl.

Combine the salsa, cream, 1 teaspoon salt and 1/2 teaspoon pepper in a blender. Process for about 30 seconds. Add to the chicken and mix well.

Heat the oil in a medium skillet over medium heat. Add the tortillas one at a time and cook each for 5 seconds on each side or until softened. Drain in a colander or on a paper towel.

Preheat the oven to 350 degrees. Mix the manchego cheese, Cotija cheese and queso fresco in a bowl. Spread a thin layer in a buttered large baking dish.

Push the chicken mixture to the side of the bowl, allowing the liquids to drain to the bottom. Dip the tortillas in the liquid to soften. Layer one-third of the tortillas and half the chicken mixture in the prepared dish. Sprinkle with half the remaining cheese mixture. Repeat the layers and top with the remaining tortillas. Cover the dish tightly with foil. Bake for 30 minutes.

Note: You can substitute a packaged three-cheese mixture for the cheeses listed above.

Chicken Enchiladas

Serves 8

1 cup chopped onion
1/2 cup chopped green bell pepper
2 tablespoons butter
3 cups shredded cooked chicken
1 (4-ounce) can chopped green chiles
1 jalapeño chile, chopped (optional)
3 tablespoons butter
1/4 cup all-purpose flour
1 teaspoon ground coriander
3/4 teaspoon salt
2 1/2 cups chicken broth
1 cup sour cream
1/2 cup (2 ounces) shredded Monterey
    Jack cheese
8 corn tortillas
1 cup (4 ounces) shredded Monterey
    Jack cheese

Preheat the oven to 350 degrees. Sauté the onion and bell pepper in 2 tablespoons butter in a saucepan until tender. Combine with the chicken, green chiles and jalapeño chile in a bowl and mix well.

Melt 3 tablespoons butter in the saucepan. Stir in the flour, coriander and salt. Add the broth all at once and stir to blend well. Cook for 1 to 2 minutes or until thickened, stirring constantly. Remove from the heat and stir in the sour cream and 1/2 cup Monterey Jack cheese. Stir 1/2 cup of the sauce into the chicken mixture.

Spoon a small amount of the sauce onto each tortilla and top with equal amounts of the chicken mixture. Roll the tortillas to enclose the filling and arrange in a lightly greased 9×13-inch baking dish. Spoon the remaining sauce over the top and sprinkle with 1 cup Monterey Jack cheese. Bake for 25 minutes.

Chicken, Corn and Black Bean Stew

Serves 8

8 ounces dried black beans

1/4 cup canola oil

11/2 pounds boneless skinless
   chicken pieces

2 ears of corn

1 onion, chopped

4 carrots, chopped

2 ribs celery, chopped

1 or 2 garlic cloves, minced

1 (16-ounce) can petite-diced tomatoes

1/4 cup tomato paste

2 pasilla chiles or poblano chiles,
   chopped

8 cups chicken broth

2 teaspoons chili powder

2 teaspoons ground cumin

2 teaspoons dried oregano

2 tablespoons chopped cilantro

Combine the beans with enough water to cover in a bowl. Let stand in the refrigerator for 8 hours; drain.

Heat the canola oil in a large skillet. Add the chicken and sauté until brown. Remove the chicken with a slotted spoon and cut into bite-size pieces. Cut the corn kernels from the ears of corn using a sharp knife.

Add the onion, carrots and celery to the drippings in the skillet. Sauté for 5 minutes. Add the garlic and sauté for 1 minute. Stir in the tomatoes, tomato paste and chiles and cook for 5 minutes.

Combine the tomato mixture with the beans, broth, chili powder, cumin and oregano in a large saucepan and mix well. Simmer for 11/4 hours. Stir in the chicken and corn and simmer until heated through. Ladle the stew into serving bowls and sprinkle with the cilantro. Serve with shredded Cheddar cheese and sour cream.

Ginger Garlic Chicken Lettuce Wraps

Serves 4 to 6

1¹/₂ pounds ground chicken breasts
6 garlic cloves, minced
¹/₂ cup finely chopped green onions
¹/₂ cup cilantro, finely chopped
2 tablespoons minced fresh gingerroot
2 teaspoons red chile flakes
¹/₄ cup sesame oil
¹/₄ cup balsamic vinegar
¹/₄ cup soy sauce
Kosher salt and freshly ground pepper
        to taste
1 head butter lettuce

Combine the chicken with the garlic, green onions, cilantro, gingerroot and red chile flakes in a bowl; mix well.

Sauté the chicken mixture in the sesame oil in a large sauté pan until partially cooked and crumbly, stirring occasionally. Add the balsamic vinegar, soy sauce, kosher salt and pepper; mix well. Cook until the chicken is cooked through and the liquid has almost completely evaporated. Separate the lettuce into leaves for the wrappers. Wrap the filling in the lettuce leaves and serve warm.

Lemon Oregano Cornish Hens

Serves 2

¹/₄ cup lemon juice
¹/₄ cup finely chopped fresh oregano
3 tablespoons minced garlic
¹/₂ tablespoon salt
¹/₂ teaspoon pepper
¹/₃ cup olive oil
2 Cornish game hens
1¹/₂ tablespoons salt
1¹/₂ teaspoons pepper

Combine the lemon juice, oregano, garlic, ¹/₂ tablespoon salt and ¹/₂ teaspoon pepper in a large bowl and whisk to mix well. Add the olive oil gradually, whisking constantly to emulsify. Add the Cornish hens and rub with the mixture to coat well. Marinate, covered, in the refrigerator for 1 to 6 hours.

Let the chicken stand at room temperature for 30 minutes or longer. Preheat the oven to 375 degrees. Drain the hens, discarding the marinade. Sprinkle the hens with 1¹/₂ tablespoons salt and 1¹/₂ teaspoons pepper and place in a baking dish. Roast for 25 to 35 minutes or to an internal temperature of 160 degrees.

Note: You can double the amount of the marinade and use half as a seasoning for potatoes to serve with the hens.

Butter-Rubbed Turkey with Apple Cider Glaze

Serves 12

1 onion, cut into quarters
6 garlic cloves
3 apples, cut into quarters
4 sprigs of fresh thyme
4 sprigs of fresh sage
1 (14- to 16-pound) turkey
1/2 cup (1 stick) butter, melted
Pepper to taste
1 cup chicken broth
2 cups apple cider
1 tablespoon all-purpose flour

Preheat the oven to 450 degrees. Place the onion, garlic, apples, thyme and sage in the cavity of the turkey. Place on a rack in a large roasting pan. Rub with the butter and season with pepper. Add the broth and apple cider to the roasting pan.

Roast the turkey for 30 minutes. Reduce the oven temperature to 350 degrees and baste with the pan juices. Roast for 2 to 2 1/2 hours or until a meat thermometer inserted in the thigh registers 165 degrees. Remove the turkey to a carving board and cover with foil. Let stand for 30 minutes.

Pour the cooking juices into a fat skimmer. Place the roasting pan over medium-high heat on the stove top. Return some of the juices to the pan and stir to loosen any brown bits from the pan. Whisk in the flour. Add the remaining juices gradually, whisking constantly and cooking until thickened. Season with pepper. Serve with the carved turkey.

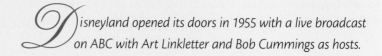

Disneyland opened its doors in 1955 with a live broadcast on ABC with Art Linkletter and Bob Cummings as hosts.

Disneyland's Blue Bayou New Orleans Crab Cakes

Serves 6

2 tablespoons butter or margarine

3 large mushrooms, minced

2 garlic cloves, minced

2 tablespoons minced onion

2 tablespoons chopped green onions

1 large shallot, minced

1 teaspoon parsley flakes

16 ounces imitation crab meat,
    finely chopped

8 ounces snow crab meat,
    finely chopped

1/2 cup bread crumbs

2 egg yolks, beaten

1 cup heavy cream

2 tablespoons cooking sherry

1 tablespoon Worcestershire sauce

1 teaspoon chicken base

1/4 teaspoon dry mustard

1/4 teaspoon thyme

1/4 teaspoon cayenne pepper

1/4 teaspoon white pepper

3 eggs, beaten

1/4 cup all-purpose flour

1/2 cup bread crumbs

Vegetable oil

Melt the butter in a sauté pan. Add the mushrooms, garlic, onion, green onions, shallot and parsley and sauté until tender. Add the imitation crab meat and snow crab meat and sauté over medium heat until heated through, stirring constantly. Add 1/2 cup bread crumbs and mix well. Stir in the egg yolks, cream, sherry, Worcestershire sauce, chicken base, dry mustard, thyme, cayenne pepper and white pepper. Spread the mixture on a baking sheet. Chill, covered, in the refrigerator for 1 hour.

Shape the crab mixture into twelve round cakes about 1/2 inch thick. Dip in the eggs and dust with the flour. Coat with 1/2 cup bread crumbs.

Preheat the oven to 350 degrees. Heat vegetable oil in a skillet until hot. Add the crab cakes and sauté until light brown on both sides. Remove to a baking dish. Bake for 10 minutes. Serve with Cajun pepper sauce and garnish with chopped fresh chives.

Lime Garlic Shrimp with Mango Mint Salsa

Serves 4

Mango Mint Salsa
2 cups chopped mangoes
3/4 cup chopped red onion
2 jalapeño chiles, seeded and chopped
1 bunch fresh mint, chopped
Juice of 1 lime

Lime Garlic Shrimp
Juice and grated zest of 1 lime
2 garlic cloves, crushed
1 tablespoon olive oil
1/2 teaspoon coarse salt
1/2 teaspoon crushed red pepper
1/4 teaspoon freshly ground black pepper
24 large shrimp, peeled and deveined

Salsa
Combine the mangoes with the onion, jalapeño chiles, mint and lime juice in a bowl and mix well. Chill in the refrigerator for 1 hour.

Shrimp
Combine the lime juice, lime zest, garlic, olive oil, coarse salt, red pepper and black pepper in a bowl and mix well. Add the shrimp and stir to coat evenly. Marinate in the refrigerator for 45 minutes.

Preheat the grill. Grill the shrimp for 2 minutes on each side or until pink. Serve with the salsa.

Grilled Shell-On Salted Shrimp

Serves 2

1 pound unpeeled shrimp, deveined
Juice of 2 or 3 lemons
Kosher salt

Combine the shrimp with the lemon juice and a generous amount of kosher salt in a sealable plastic bag. Marinate in the refrigerator for 10 to 15 minutes.

Preheat the grill to medium heat. Place the shrimp in a grill basket and grill until firm, turning once. Serve hot with plenty of napkins and a bowl for the shells.

Note: This makes a delicious meal when served with boiled potatoes and fresh corn on the cob. You may also serve as an appetizer.

Claes's Bouillabaisse

Serves 1

1/2 lobster tail
1 tablespoon vegetable oil
2 shrimp
1 fish fillet
4 mussels
4 clams
1/4 cup white wine
1 baby carrot, chopped
1 baby fennel bulb, chopped
2 fingerling potatoes, chopped
2 cups Bouillabaisse Broth
    (page 115)
Salt and pepper to taste
1 slice bread, toasted
1 tablespoon Rouille (page 115)

Remove the meat from the lobster tail. Heat the oil to the smoke point in a sauté pan. Add the lobster and shrimp carefully to the sauté pan and sauté until the bottom is caramelized. Turn the seafood and add the fish, mussels and clams.

Add the wine, stirring up the brown bits from the sauté pan and shaking the pan frequently to prevent burning. Cook until the wine has reduced and the alcohol has evaporated. Add the carrot, fennel, potatoes and Bouillabaise Broth. Reduce the heat and cover. Cook until the mussel shells have opened. Season with salt and pepper. Top with the toast and Rouille to serve.

Claes Restaurant is a fine-dining experience complemented by an unrivaled panoramic view of the Pacific Ocean, signature seafood dishes, prime steak dishes, and an award-winning wine cellar. Located in the Hotel Laguna in Laguna Beach, Claes has been a local favorite for its relaxing atmosphere and excellent service.

Bouillabaise Broth

Makes 1 gallon

6 cloves of garlic
1/4 cup extra-virgin olive oil
1 fennel bulb, chopped
1 onion, chopped
1 leek, chopped
8 canned tomatoes
3/4 cup white wine
4 ounces clams
4 ounces mussels
1 pound fish bones
Grated zest of 1/2 orange
1/4 bunch thyme
1/4 bunch parsley
1 bay leaf
1/4 tablespoon saffron

Cook the garlic in the olive oil in a large stockpot until roasted. Add the fennel, onion, leek and tomatoes and sweat until tender. Add the wine, clams, mussels, fish bones, orange zest, thyme, parsley, bay leaf and saffron. Add enough water to cover the ingredients. Bring to a boil and cook for 20 minutes. Strain the mixture into a 1-gallon container and chill in the refrigerator, discarding the solids.

Rouille

Makes 4 cups

4 red bell peppers, roasted, peeled
    and seeded
6 garlic cloves, boiled
7 slices white bread, soaked in olive oil
Lemon juice to taste
Salt to taste

Combine the bell peppers, garlic, bread, lemon juice and salt in a blender and process until smooth. Store in an airtight container in the refrigerator.

John Stamos's Marinated Grilled Seafood

Serves 8

1 cup olive oil

1/4 cup white wine

3 tablespoons fresh lemon juice

6 garlic cloves, minced

1 tablespoon dried oregano

1 teaspoon salt

1 pound large shrimp, peeled
     and deveined

1 1/4 pounds sea scallops

Salt and pepper to taste

Combine the olive oil, wine, lemon juice, garlic, oregano and 1 teaspoon salt in a jar with a lid and shake to mix well. Combine with the shrimp and scallops in a sealable plastic bag. Marinate in the refrigerator for 2 hours, turning the bag occasionally. Soak eight wooden skewers in water in a bowl for 30 minutes.

Preheat a charcoal grill or gas grill to high heat. Drain the skewers and seafood, discarding the marinade. Thread the shrimp and scallops onto the skewers. Season with salt and pepper. Grill for 6 to 8 minutes or until opaque.

A native of Cypress, California, John Stamos began his career on the soap opera General Hospital. *Stamos rose to fame with the role of Jesse on the hit television show* Full House *and again as Dr. Tony Gates on* ER. *In addition to appearing on numerous television programs and movies, Stamos has also played drums with The Beach Boys and starred on Broadway. His movie star good looks and charming personality have made him one of Orange County's favorite sons.*

Halibut with Mushroom Olive Sauce

Serves 6

1 tablespoon olive oil
1 small onion, cut into thin wedges
1 garlic clove, minced
1 (15-ounce) can diced tomatoes
1 cup sliced cremini mushrooms or
    button mushrooms
3/4 cup coarsely chopped pimento-
    stuffed green olives
1 tablespoon chopped fresh oregano, or
    1/2 teaspoon dried oregano
1/4 teaspoon salt
1/8 teaspoon freshly ground pepper
6 (4-ounce) halibut fillets

Heat the olive oil in a large skillet over medium heat. Add the onion and garlic and sauté for 2 to 3 minutes or until the onion is tender. Add the undrained tomatoes, mushrooms, olives, oregano, salt and pepper. Bring to a boil.

Add the halibut carefully to the skillet and spoon the sauce over the top. Return to a boil. Reduce the heat and simmer, covered, for 8 to 10 minutes or until the fish flakes easily with a fork. Lift the fish to a serving platter using a wide spatula. Spoon the sauce over the fish and serve with rice and/or crusty bread.

Salmon with Dungeness Crab à la Balboa

Serves 4

1 pound Dungeness crab meat
2 bunches green onions, chopped
1/2 cup bread crumbs
1/4 cup mayonnaise
1/4 cup (1/2 stick) butter, melted
1 egg, beaten
1 tablespoon Old Bay seasoning
1 tablespoon dry mustard
Salt and pepper to taste
4 (6-ounce) salmon steaks
1 tablespoon olive oil
1 tablespoon butter

Preheat the oven to 375 degrees. Combine the crab meat, green onions, bread crumbs, mayonnaise, 1/4 cup melted butter, the egg, Old Bay seasoning, dry mustard, salt and pepper in a large bowl and mix well. Spoon the mixture onto the salmon steaks.

Combine the olive oil with 1 tablespoon butter in a roasting pan. Heat in the oven. Remove from the oven and carefully add the fish. Bake for 15 to 20 minutes or until the fish flakes easily with a fork. Garnish with lemon wedges, capers and parsley to serve.

Five Crowns' Black Pepper-Crusted Salmon with Pea Shoots and Cream Sauce

Serves 4

Cream Sauce

2 teaspoons chopped shallot
1 tablespoon butter
1 cup heavy cream
Salt and white pepper to taste

Black Pepper-Crusted Salmon with Pea Shoots

4 (8-ounce) salmon fillets, 1 inch thick
1 tablespoon vegetable oil
Salt to taste
2 tablespoons coarsely cracked
    black pepper
8 cups salted water
4 cups pea shoots

Sauce

Sauté the shallot in the butter in a small saucepan until translucent. Add the cream and return to a simmer. Simmer until reduced to a thick-pouring sauce consistency. Season with salt and white pepper. Keep warm.

Salmon

Preheat the oven to 425 degrees. Brush the salmon with the oil and season with the salt and black pepper. Place on a nonstick baking sheet in the upper third of the oven. Bake for 7 to 9 minutes or until the fish flakes easily with a fork.

Bring the water to a boil in a large saucepan and add the pea shoots. Cook for 30 seconds; drain in a colander. Spoon onto four serving plates.

Place the fish on the pea shoots and spoon the cream sauce around the plates. Garnish the plates with mint oil.

This recipe is from Five Crowns' Executive Chef Dennis Brask. Five Crowns is a beautiful replica of one of England's oldest country inns and is known for excellent prime rib and lighter seasonal menus. A place of cozy fireplaces and warm hospitality, it delights the eye with antiques and rare paintings in its distinctive rooms and sunlit greenhouse, each with its own charming character. Here you will find the award-winning food, outstanding wine list, exceptional service, and unmistakable style that have made this Lawry's restaurant a dining legend since 1965.

Wild Salmon with Fresh Mint and Blackberries

Serves 2

1/2 cup fresh mint leaves
2 (6-ounce) wild salmon fillets
2 to 3 tablespoons olive oil
1 cup fresh blackberries
2 to 3 tablespoons blackberry vinegar
    or raspberry vinegar
Hot cooked rice or salad greens

Preheat the oven to 350 degrees. Stack and roll the mint leaves. Cut into thin slices.

Coat the salmon lightly with the olive oil. Place in a baking dish and top with the mint and blackberries. Sprinkle lightly with the blackberry vinegar and cover with foil.

Bake for 15 to 20 minutes or until the fish flakes easily with a fork. Serve hot over rice or chill and serve over a salad for lunch.

Note: You can also wrap the salmon in foil and grill.

Grilled Salmon with Chilled Cucumber Sauce

Serves 2

2 (8-ounce) salmon fillets
1 English cucumber, peeled, seeded
    and chopped
Juice of 1 lime
3/4 cup fresh cilantro, chopped
3 tablespoons Greek-style low-fat yogurt
Pinch of kosher salt
Pinch of cayenne pepper
2 sprigs of fresh dill weed
Mixed greens

Preheat the grill. Grill the salmon for 10 minutes for each inch of thickness. Cool to room temperature; chill in the refrigerator for 1 hour.

Combine the cucumber, lime juice, cilantro, yogurt, kosher salt and cayenne pepper in a blender. Pulse until smooth. Spoon into a bowl and chill in the refrigerator.

Serve the fish over a bed of mixed greens and top with the dill weed. Serve with the cucumber sauce.

Grilled Salmon with Cilantro-Jalapeño Pesto

Serves 4

Cilantro-Jalapeño Pesto
1 cup extra-virgin olive oil
1 cup chopped cilantro
1 garlic clove
Juice of 1 lime
1 jalapeño chile (or to taste), chopped
Kosher salt and freshly ground pepper
     to taste

Grilled Salmon
4 (6-ounce) salmon fillets
Extra-virgin olive oil

Pesto
Combine the olive oil with the cilantro and garlic in a small food processor and process until smooth. Mix with the lime juice, jalapeño chile, kosher salt and pepper in a bowl.

Salmon
Preheat the grill to high heat. Brush the salmon lightly with olive oil. Grill for 4 minutes on each side or until cooked through. Serve with the pesto.

Maple-Glazed Salmon

Serves 4

3 tablespoons maple syrup
2 tablespoons soy sauce
1 green onion, thinly sliced
1 teaspoon ground ginger
4 (6-ounce) salmon fillets

Preheat the grill. Combine the maple syrup, soy sauce, green onion and ginger in a small bowl and whisk to mix well. Brush on the salmon. Place the fish skin side down on the grill. Grill for 8 to 12 minutes or until the fish flakes easily with a fork, basting several times.

Sea Bass with Avocado Lime Salsa

Serves 2

Sea Bass

2 sea bass fillets
1 to 2 tablespoons olive oil
Juice of 1/2 lime
Salt and pepper to taste

Avocado Lime Salsa

1 avocado, chopped
1 bunch chives, chopped
1/4 cup olive oil
Juice of 1/2 lime
Salt and pepper to taste

Sea Bass

Rinse the sea bass and pat dry. Rub with the olive oil and drizzle with the lime juice. Let stand for several minutes.

Preheat the broiler. Place the fish on a baking sheet lined with foil. Season with salt and pepper. Broil for 15 minutes or just until opaque; do not turn. Keep warm.

Salsa

Combine the avocado, chives, olive oil and lime juice in a bowl. Season with salt and pepper and mix gently. Serve with the fish.

Red Snapper Veracruz

Serves 8

1 1/2 pounds red snapper fillets
1/2 cup lime juice
1/2 teaspoon salt, or to taste
2 tablespoons olive oil
1 small onion, chopped
1 small green bell pepper, cut into strips
1 1/2 teaspoons minced garlic
1/2 cup dry white wine
1 (16-ounce) jar thick-and-chunky salsa
1/2 cup tomato sauce
1/4 cup sliced jalapeño chiles
1/4 cup black olives
1 tablespoon capers
1 tablespoon chopped cilantro

Arrange the snapper in a shallow dish. Sprinkle with the lime juice and salt. Marinate, covered, in the refrigerator for 20 minutes or longer.

Heat the olive oil in a large nonstick skillet over medium-high heat. Add the onion, bell pepper and garlic and sauté for 1 to 2 minutes or until the vegetables are tender-crisp. Stir in the wine and cook for 1 minute.

Add the salsa, tomato sauce, jalapeño chiles, black olives and capers. Bring to a boil. Place the fish in the skillet and reduce the heat to low. Simmer, covered, for 8 to 10 minutes or until the fish flakes easily with a fork. Sprinkle with the cilantro and garnish with lime wedges.

Note: You may substitute halibut fillets for the snapper in this dish.

Amelia's Lady Sole with Claire Amandine Sauce

Serves 6

Lady Sole
1 egg, beaten
1 cup milk
12 small sole fillets
1 1/2 cups fine bread crumbs
18 scallops, chopped
1/4 cup (1/2 stick) butter, melted

Claire Amandine Sauce
1/2 cup (1 stick) butter
1/2 cup all-purpose flour
1 cup sautéed sliced mushrooms
1 1/2 cups cooked Alaskan king crab meat
Salt and pepper to taste
1 cup (4 ounces) shredded
    Cheddar cheese
1 tablespoon chopped chives
1 tablespoon chopped parsley
1 cup semidry sherry
1/4 cup toasted sliced almonds

Sole

Preheat the oven to 350 degrees. Whisk the egg and milk in a bowl until smooth. Dip the fillets into the egg mixture and coat with the bread crumbs. Reserve the remaining egg mixture for the sauce. Arrange the fillets in a baking pan. Spoon the chopped scallops onto six of the fillets. Brush with the butter. Broil for 12 minutes. Place the plain fillets on top of the scallop-topped fillets.

Sauce

Melt the butter in a saucepan and whisk in the flour. Add the mushrooms, crab meat, salt and pepper. Stir in the cheese, chives, parsley, sherry and reserved egg and milk mixture. Cook until thickened, stirring constantly; do not boil. Serve over the fish and sprinkle with the almonds.

For nearly fifty years, Amelia's Seafood and Italian Restaurant on Balboa Island has offered a distinct menu of delectable Italian and seafood dishes, many of which are original recipes from the kitchen of Amelia Seton, a native of Italy and the founder of Amelia's. In 1961, when Amelia started the restaurant, Milton Bren and Claire Trevor were avid patrons. In appreciation of their support, Amelia created Lady Sole with Claire Sauce for Mrs. Bren.

Tilapia with Coconut-Almond Crust

Serves 2

Mango Salsa

1 cup chopped mango
2 tablespoons chopped red onion
1 tablespoon chopped seeded
    jalapeño chile
1 tablespoon olive oil
Juice of 1 lime
1 teaspoon chopped fresh mint

Tilapia with Coconut-Almond Crust

3 tablespoons unsweetened
    shredded coconut
2 tablespoons chopped almonds
1/4 cup plain yogurt
1 teaspoon minced garlic
1 teaspoon grated gingerroot
1 teaspoon grated lime zest
Pinch of coarse salt
Pinch of freshly ground pepper
2 tilapia fillets

Salsa

Combine the mango, onion, jalapeño chile, olive oil, lime juice and mint in a small bowl and mix well.

Tilapia

Preheat the oven to 350 degrees. Mix the coconut and almonds in a small bowl. Combine the yogurt, garlic, gingerroot, lime zest, coarse salt and pepper in a shallow nonreactive dish.

Dip the tilapia in the yogurt mixture and arrange in a baking dish. Press the coconut mixture over the fish. Bake for 18 to 20 minutes or until the fish is opaque and cooked through. Serve warm with the salsa.

Tilapia with Salsa Verde Glaze

Serves 4

1/4 cup mayonnaise
1/4 cup salsa verde
1 garlic clove, minced
1 teaspoon minced chipotle chile
Juice of 1/2 lime
Pepper to taste
1 1/3 pounds tilapia fillets
1 tablespoon chopped cilantro

Combine the mayonnaise, salsa verde, garlic, chipotle chile, lime juice and pepper in a bowl and mix well for the glaze.

Preheat the oven to 425 degrees. Arrange the tilapia in a baking pan sprayed with nonstick cooking spray. Spread the glaze evenly over the top. Bake for 10 to 12 minutes or until cooked through. Sprinkle with the cilantro.

Fish in Foil

Serves 4

Olive oil
1 onion, chopped
1 potato, sliced
4 (4-ounce) salmon fillets
1/4 cup pesto
Kernels from 1 ear of corn
Snap peas
1/4 cup goat cheese
1/4 cup pine nuts
Splash of chardonnay or sauvignon blanc

Preheat the grill. Prepare four squares of foil large enough to completely enclose the ingredients. Place on a work surface and brush with olive oil. Sprinkle the onion into the centers of the foil squares and top with the potato slices.

Arrange one salmon fillet over the potatoes in each foil square and brush evenly with the pesto. Layer the corn, snap peas, goat cheese and pine nuts over the fish. Drizzle each with a small amount of the wine. Seal the foil packet tightly. Grill the packets for 30 minutes or until done to taste.

Note: Use a knife or mandoline to slice the potatoes thick enough to retain their shape under the salmon as they cook. You can prepare the packets in advance and store in the refrigerator until grilling time. You can substitute tapenade for the pesto and/or any white fish for the salmon.

Opah's Peppercorn Sesame Ahi with Mango Vegetable Slaw

Serves 4

Mango Vegetable Slaw

1 mango, julienned
1 red bell pepper, julienned
1 yellow bell pepper, julienned
1 zucchini, julienned
1 jalapeño chile, seeded and
    finely chopped
1/2 red onion, julienned
1 bunch green onions, sliced diagonally
1 bunch cilantro, chopped
1 cup rice vinegar
1/4 cup wild honey

Thai Citrus Broth

1 cup soy sauce
Juice of 1 orange
1/2 cup rice vinegar
1/4 cup wild honey
2 garlic cloves, finely chopped
Juice of 1 lime
1 tablespoon finely chopped gingerroot
Pinch of red pepper flakes
1/2 cup orange juice
Cornstarch

Peppercorn Sesame Ahi

4 (6-ounce) blocks fresh first-grade ahi tuna
Salt and pepper to taste
1/2 cup sesame seeds
1 tablespoon cracked peppercorns
1/2 cup olive oil

Slaw

Combine the mango, red bell pepper, yellow bell pepper, zucchini, jalapeño chile, red onion, green onions and cilantro in a bowl. Add the rice vinegar and honey and toss to coat evenly.

Citrus Broth

Combine the soy sauce, juice of 1 orange, the rice vinegar, honey, garlic, lime juice, gingerroot and red pepper flakes in a saucepan and mix well. Bring to a slow simmer over low heat. Blend 1/2 cup orange juice with enough cornstarch to make the sauce the desired consistency in a small bowl. Whisk into the sauce mixture and cook until thickened. Keep warm.

Ahi

Season the ahi with salt and pepper. Mix the sesame seeds and cracked peppercorns together. Roll the fish in the sesame seed mixture, coating evenly.

Heat the olive oil to the smoke point in a sauté pan. Add the fish and sear evenly on all sides. Remove to a cutting board and let stand for 2 to 3 minutes. Cut each block into five to seven slices with a very sharp knife.

Serve with the slaw and citrus broth. Add coconut rice or wasabi mashed potatoes and baby bok choy, asparagus, or rappini to make it a meal.

The opah, or moonfish, was once viewed as good luck when caught by fishermen and was often given away as a gesture of good will. For a truly unforgettable dining experience, visit Opah Restaurant and Bar in Aliso Viejo or Irvine, where the modern and streamlined design, eclectic fare, and bustling martini bar are both inviting and innovative.

Antonello's Seafood Linguini

Serves 4

12 cups water
Salt to taste
16 ounces linguini
1/4 cup extra-virgin olive oil
4 whole dried red chiles
2 teaspoons coarsely chopped garlic
1/2 cup chopped green onions
1/2 cup fresh basil, chopped
1/2 cup fresh Italian parsley, chopped
2 teaspoons dried oregano
1 teaspoon salt
1 teaspoon freshly ground pepper
6 ounces fresh fish, chopped
6 ounces shrimp, peeled and deveined
4 cups crushed tomatoes
1 cup clam juice
1/2 cup dry white wine

Bring the water to a boil in a stockpot and season with salt to taste. Add the pasta and cook for 8 to 9 minutes or until tender. Drain well and keep warm.

Heat the olive oil in a large saucepan. Add the red chiles and garlic. Sauté until golden brown. Add the green onions, basil, parsley, oregano, 1 teaspoon salt and the pepper. Sauté for 1 to 2 minutes.

Add the fish and shrimp. Sauté for 2 minutes, stirring frequently. Stir in the tomatoes, clam juice and wine. Cook over low heat for 10 minutes. Combine with the pasta in a bowl and toss to mix well.

Since 1979, Santa Ana's award-winning Antonello Ristorante has captured the essence of the Old World authenticity with a new cuisine—Cucina Nostalgica Italiana. The Italian dishes, made with the freshest ingredients, are created by Executive Chef Barone, with occasional assistance from proprietor Antonio Cagnolo's mother, Mama Pina.

Four-Cheese Lasagna

Serves 8

1/2 cup (1 stick) butter
1/4 cup all-purpose flour
1 cup milk
1 cup chicken broth
Salt to taste
1 egg
8 ounces ricotta cheese
1/4 cup (1 ounce) grated Parmesan cheese
Pinch of nutmeg
1/2 teaspoon salt
1 pound ground beef or ground turkey
1/2 cup chopped onion
3 garlic cloves, minced
1 tablespoon olive oil
3 pounds large tomatoes, peeled, seeded
    and chopped (about 6 or 7)
2 tablespoons chopped fresh parsley
2 tablespoons chopped fresh basil
1/2 teaspoon oregano
1 1/2 teaspoons salt
1/4 teaspoon freshly ground pepper
8 ounces lasagna noodles
1 1/2 cups (6 ounces) grated
    Parmesan cheese
4 ounces mozzarella cheese, sliced
4 ounces Teleme cheese or Monterey
    Jack cheese, shredded
Butter

Melt 1/2 cup butter in a saucepan. Add the flour and cook for 1 minute, whisking constantly. Add the milk and broth gradually and bring to a boil, whisking constantly. Season with salt to taste.

Beat the egg in a bowl. Add the ricotta cheese, 1/4 cup Parmesan cheese, the nutmeg and 1/2 teaspoon salt; mix well with a fork.

Sauté the ground beef with the onion and garlic in the olive oil in a saucepan until the beef is brown and crumbly; drain. Add the tomatoes, parsley, basil, oregano, 1 1/2 teaspoons salt and the pepper; mix well. Cook over medium-low to medium heat for 30 to 40 minutes or until thick. Skim any fat from the surface.

Preheat the oven to 400 degrees. Cook the lasagna noodles al dente in boiling salted water. Drain and place in cold water to prevent sticking.

Spread a small amount of the meat sauce in a lightly greased 9×13-inch baking dish. Arrange half the noodles in the prepared dish and layer half the remaining meat sauce, 1/2 cup of the broth mixture, 1/2 cup of the Parmesan cheese, half the mozzarella cheese, half the Teleme cheese and half the ricotta filling over the noodles. Top with the remaining noodles.

Layer with the remaining meat sauce, 1/2 cup of the broth mixture, 1/2 cup of the Parmesan cheese, and the remaining mozzarella cheese, Teleme cheese and ricotta filling. Top with the remaining broth mixture and Parmesan cheese. Dot with butter. Bake for 30 to 40 minutes or until bubbly.

Note: You can prepare the lasagna in advance and store in the refrigerator or freezer until needed. You can substitute chopped drained canned tomatoes for the fresh tomatoes. You can also substitute 1 teaspoon parsley flakes and 1 teaspoon dried basil for the fresh parsley and basil.

Spaghetti and Meatballs

Serves 12 to 15

Meat Sauce

2 pounds Italian sausages
1 cup chopped onion
4 garlic cloves, minced
3 tablespoons olive oil
3 (28-ounce) cans crushed tomatoes
3 (28-ounce) cans tomato purée
2 (8-ounce) cans tomato sauce
1 cup red wine
2 tablespoons chopped fresh basil,
    or to taste
2 tablespoons chopped fresh oregano,
    or to taste
2 tablespoons parsley flakes
1 tablespoon salt, or to taste

Sauce

Remove and discard the casings from half the sausages; crumble the sausage. Cut the remaining sausages into halves. Sauté the onion and garlic in the olive oil in a saucepan. Add the sausage and sauté until brown. Add the tomatoes, tomato purée, tomato sauce, wine, basil, oregano, parsley and salt and mix well. Simmer for 2 hours or longer.

Meatballs

12 ounces ground beef
12 ounces ground pork
1 cup bread crumbs
1/2 cup (2 ounces) grated Parmesan cheese
1/2 cup milk
2 eggs, beaten
1 garlic clove, minced
1 tablespoon parsley
1 1/2 teaspoons salt
1/4 teaspoon pepper

Meatballs

Combine the ground beef, ground pork, bread crumbs and Parmesan cheese in a large bowl. Add the milk, eggs, garlic, parsley, salt and pepper. Mix well with your hands. Shape into 2-inch meatballs and place in a broiler pan. Broil until brown, turning once, or sauté in a small amount of oil in a skillet until brown. Add to the sauce and simmer until cooked through and ready to serve.

Assembly

16 ounces spaghetti
Grated Parmesan cheese to taste

Assembly

Cook the pasta using the package directions; drain and rinse. Spoon into a serving bowl and top with the meatballs and sauce. Sprinkle with Parmesan cheese.

130

Chris Pronger's Spaghetti Spinach Bake

Serves 6

2 cups sliced mushrooms
3/4 cup chopped onion
1/3 cup vegetable oil
1 (10-ounce) package frozen chopped
    spinach, thawed and drained
16 ounces low-fat cottage cheese
Garlic powder to taste
1/4 teaspoon nutmeg
1/2 teaspoon salt
1/4 teaspoon pepper
8 ounces thin spaghetti, cooked
    and drained
1 cup (4 ounces) shredded
    mozzarella cheese

Preheat the oven to 425 degrees. Sauté the mushrooms and onion in the oil in a large skillet for 5 minutes or until tender. Stir in the spinach. Sauté for 2 minutes. Add the cottage cheese, garlic powder, nutmeg, salt and pepper. Combine with the spaghetti in a bowl and toss to mix well.

Spoon into an oiled 6×10-inch baking dish and top with the mozzarella cheese. Bake, covered, for 20 minutes or until heated through and the cheese melts.

Anaheim Ducks' defenseman and team captain Chris Pronger is a legend in the National Hockey League. Originally selected second overall in the draft by the Hartford Whalers in 1993, he has also played for the St. Louis Blues and the Edmonton Oilers. He was the 1999–2000 Hart Trophy winner and was instrumental in helping Canada capture the gold at the 2002 Olympics and in leading the Ducks to win the Stanley Cup Championship in 2007.

Palm Terrace's Macaroni and Cheese with Crushed Truffle and Taleggio Sauce

Serves 4

3 button mushrooms, sliced

2 shallots, chopped

2 garlic cloves, minced

1/4 rib celery, chopped

1/4 cup chopped leek
    (white portion only)

2 tablespoons butter

1 1/2 cups chablis or other white wine

3 cups heavy cream

3 or 4 sprigs of thyme

1 bay leaf

18 white peppercorns

16 ounces Taleggio cheese, cut into pieces

1/4 cup (1 ounce) grated Reggiano cheese

2 tablespoons crushed truffles

2 teaspoons white truffle oil

1 teaspoon black truffle oil

Salt and freshly ground pepper to taste

4 cups elbow macaroni, cooked
    and chilled

1 tablespoon chopped chives

Sweat the mushrooms, shallots, garlic, celery and leek in the butter in a saucepan over medium heat until tender, but not brown. Add the wine and bring to a simmer. Cook until most of the wine has evaporated. Stir in the cream and bring to a simmer. Add the thyme, bay leaf and peppercorns. Simmer for 20 minutes to reduce slightly.

Stir in the Taleggio cheese and Reggiano cheese and remove from the heat. Remove the bay leaf and thyme sprigs. Process the sauce in a blender until smooth. Strain into a large saucepan.

Heat the sauce over low heat. Add the truffles, white truffle oil and black truffle oil. Season with salt and pepper. Add the pasta and mix well. Simmer until heated through. Sprinkle with the chives and serve hot.

Note: You can add variety to this dish with the addition of lobster or shrimp.

Acclaimed Chef Bill Bracken spearheads Island Hotel's signature restaurant, Palm Terrace, showcasing his innovative American-style cuisine, including his "small bites" menu. Signature dinner items include Potato-Crusted Black Cod; Roasted Kurobuta Pork; and Thirty-Hour Kobe Short Ribs. Executive Pastry Chef Michael Owens presides over desserts and offers such sinful treats as homemade Snickers ice cream served with a butterscotch brownie; caramelized bananas; and caramel, chocolate, and vanilla sauces. It is open daily from 6:30 in the morning to 10:00 at night.

Savory Macaroni and Cheese

Serves 12

4 slices whole wheat bread, trimmed
2 tablespoons butter, melted
1/4 cup (1/2 stick) butter
1/2 cup all-purpose flour
5 cups milk
2 teaspoons kosher salt
1/4 teaspoon ground nutmeg
1/4 teaspoon cayenne pepper
1/4 teaspoon freshly ground black pepper
16 ounces sharp white Cheddar
    cheese, shredded
8 ounces Romano cheese or Gruyère
    cheese, grated
16 ounces multigrain elbow macaroni,
    cooked al dente and drained

Preheat the oven to 375 degrees. Tear the bread into large pieces and place in a food processor. Pulse just until the bread is coarsely processed into 1/4-inch pieces. Place in a small bowl and drizzle with 2 tablespoons melted butter; toss to mix well.

Melt 1/4 cup butter in a large skillet with high sides over medium heat. Stir in the flour. Cook for 1 to 2 minutes, stirring constantly. Add the milk 1 cup at a time. Cook for 20 to 30 minutes or until thickened, whisking constantly. Season with the kosher salt, nutmeg, cayenne pepper and black pepper. Remove from the heat.

Mix the Cheddar cheese and Romano cheese in a bowl. Reserve 2 cups of the cheese mixture. Stir the remaining cheese into the sauce until melted. Add the pasta and toss to mix well.

Spoon the pasta mixture into a buttered baking dish. Sprinkle with the reserved 2 cups cheese and the buttered bread crumbs. Bake for 30 minutes or until the top is brown and crunchy. Cool for 5 to 10 minutes before serving. Serve with Tabasco sauce for an extra spicy "kick."

Penne Arrabbiata

Serves 4

3 cups penne
12 garlic cloves, minced
2 teaspoons red pepper flakes
1/2 cup olive oil
1 cup (4 ounces) shaved Parmesan cheese
1/4 cup minced flat-leaf parsley
2 cups chopped seeded fresh tomatoes

Cook the pasta using the package directions; drain and place in a large serving bowl. Sauté the garlic and red pepper flakes in the olive oil in a saucepan over low heat. Add to the pasta and toss to mix well. Add half the Parmesan cheese and the parsley and toss lightly. Add the tomatoes and season with salt and pepper; mix well. Top with the remaining Parmesan cheese.

Note: For a heartier dinner, marinate chicken or shrimp in olive oil infused with garlic, basil and/or red pepper. Sauté and toss with the pasta before adding the tomatoes.

133

Whole Wheat Penne with Pistachios and Asparagus

Serves 6 to 8

1/2 cup pistachios

Salt to taste

1 pound thin asparagus spears,
    cut into thirds

2 garlic cloves, cut into halves

1/4 cup olive oil

1/4 teaspoon freshly ground pepper

1/3 cup dry white wine

1 cup half-and-half

1/4 cup heavy cream

1 1/2 teaspoons kosher salt

16 ounces whole wheat penne

1/2 cup (2 ounces) grated
    Parmesan cheese

Preheat the oven to 350 degrees. Sprinkle the pistachios on a baking sheet. Toast in the oven for 5 minutes. Cool and chop the pistachios.

Bring a large saucepan of salted water to a boil. Add the asparagus and cook for 3 minutes or until tender-crisp. Remove to a bowl with a slotted spoon, reserving the cooking liquid.

Sauté the garlic lightly in the olive oil in a small sauté pan over medium heat. Press the garlic with a wooden spoon to release its flavor. Sauté until the garlic begins to brown; remove and discard the garlic.

Add the asparagus and pepper to the sauté pan. Increase the heat to high and add the wine. Cook for 1 minute, stirring constantly. Reduce the heat to medium. Add the half-and-half and cream. Simmer for 3 minutes. Season with the kosher salt and keep warm.

Cook the pasta in the reserved water using the package directions. Drain the pasta and return to the saucepan. Add the asparagus sauce and mix well. Cook over low heat until heated through. Stir in the Parmesan cheese. Sprinkle with the toasted pistachios to serve.

Note: For a heartier dish, add cooked bacon or prosciutto.

Porcini Risotto

Serves 4 to 6

2 ounces dried porcini
2 bunches green onions, chopped
3 carrots, minced
1/4 cup (1/2 stick) butter
2 cups arborio rice
1/2 cup dry white wine
4 to 5 cups beef stock
16 ounces mushrooms, sliced
1/4 cup (1/2 stick) butter
3 garlic cloves, minced
3/4 cup parsley, minced
Salt and pepper to taste
1 cup (4 ounces) grated Parmesan cheese
1 cup heavy cream or milk
2 eggs
Pinch of nutmeg
1/2 cup (2 ounces) grated
    Parmesan cheese

Combine the porcini with enough hot water to cover in a bowl; let stand for 30 minutes. Drain, reserving the porcini and liquid.

Sauté the green onions and carrots in 1/4 cup butter in a skillet for 10 minutes. Add the rice and sauté for 1 minute. Add the reserved porcini liquid, the wine and enough of the stock to just cover the rice. Simmer over low heat for 30 minutes or until the rice is tender, adding additional stock as it is absorbed by the rice and stirring frequently.

Sauté the porcini and fresh mushrooms in 1/4 cup butter in a medium skillet for 10 minutes. Add the garlic, parsley, salt and pepper. Cook over low heat for 10 minutes.

Preheat the oven to 350 degrees. Spread half the rice in a buttered 2-quart baking dish. Top with the mushrooms and 1 cup Parmesan cheese. Spread with the remaining rice.

Combine the cream, eggs and nutmeg in a bowl and beat until smooth. Pour over the rice and sprinkle with 1/2 cup Parmesan cheese. Bake for 30 minutes or until puffed and golden brown. Let stand for several minutes to cool slightly before serving.

South County

BRUNCH

Orange County is unique in that there is no city center. Because of this, residents tend to divide the county in two, North Orange County and South County. It is a distinction that has come to differentiate the older areas of the county that are closer to Los Angeles and the more recently developed areas that are to the South and East. Cities such as Mission Viejo, Laguna Niguel, Rancho Santa Margarita, and Aliso Viejo were incorporated as recently as 2001. They stand as a testament to the growth Orange County has seen since its inception in 1889. South County is not without historical significance, however.

The Mission San Juan Capistrano is one of the historical gems in Orange County. Founded on November 1, 1776, by Padre Junipero Serra, the Mission is one of California's most important historical, cultural, and educational centers. It is also home to the famous swallows of San Juan Capistrano. Each year the Mission hosts The Swallows Festival, celebrating their return on March 19.

South County was also home to President Richard Nixon's Western White House. In 1969 President Nixon bought La Casa Pacifica overlooking the Pacific Ocean in San Clemente. His presence put San Clemente on the map, so to speak, and this beautiful little beach town is now a popular tourist and surfing destination.

Though much of South County's history is young, it has quickly become one of the hottest places to live in The OC. From the mountains to the ocean, there is something for everyone in South County.

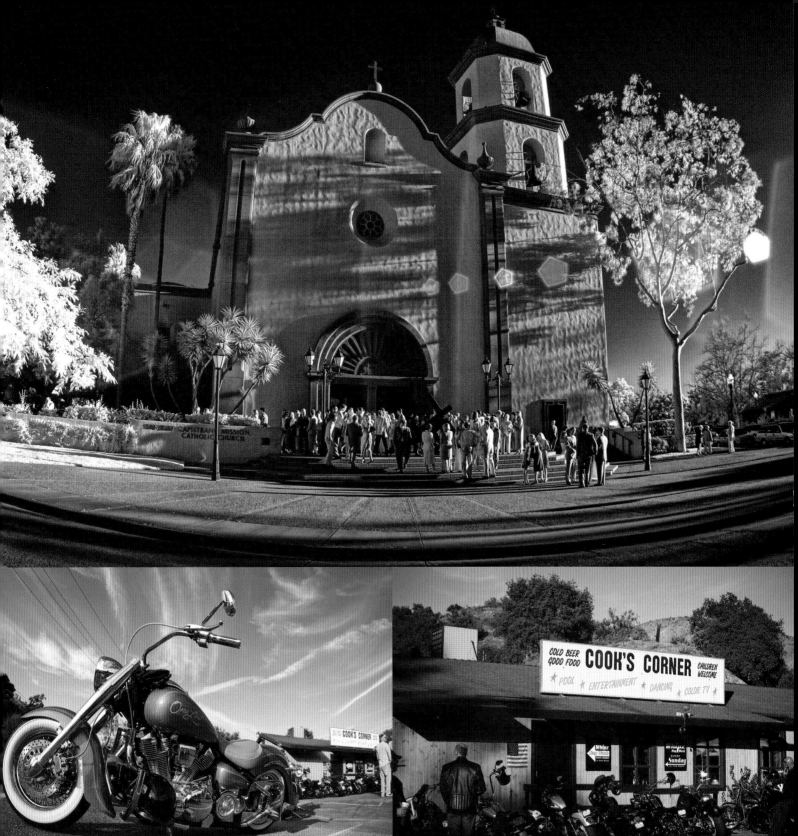

Spinach and Chicken Crepes

Serves 8 to 10

Crepes

1/4 cup (1/2 stick) butter, melted
4 eggs
2 cups milk
1 cup sifted all-purpose flour
1/4 teaspoon grated fresh nutmeg
1 teaspoon salt
Melted butter for brushing

Chicken and Spinach Filling

1/2 cup (1 stick) butter
16 ounces mushrooms, finely chopped
2 large onions, finely chopped
4 cups chopped cooked chicken
2 pounds fresh spinach, chopped,
    or 2 (10-ounce) packages
    frozen chopped spinach,
    thawed and drained
1 cup sour cream
1/4 cup dry sherry
1 teaspoon salt
Pinch of cayenne pepper

Sherry Cheese Sauce

1/2 cup (1 stick) butter
1/2 cup sifted all-purpose flour
4 cups fresh or canned chicken stock
2 cups milk
1 cup dry sherry
1 cup (4 ounces) grated Parmesan cheese
1 cup (4 ounces) shredded Swiss cheese

Crepes

Combine 1/4 cup butter, eggs, milk, flour, nutmeg and salt in a blender and process until smooth. Chill in the refrigerator for 2 hours.

Heat a 6- or 7-inch crepe pan over medium heat and brush lightly with butter. Ladle 2 tablespoons of the crepe batter at a time into the crepe pan and tilt the pan to cover the surface evenly. Cook for 1 minute or until light brown on the bottom. Turn the crepe and cook just until light brown on the other side. Stack the crepes between layers of waxed paper. Use immediately or store in the refrigerator or freezer until needed. Thaw frozen crepes before filling.

Filling

Melt the butter in a heavy skillet and add the mushrooms and onions; sauté until tender, increasing the heat for 1 minute if needed to evaporate the moisture from the mushrooms. Add the chicken, spinach, sour cream, sherry, salt and cayenne pepper. Cook until heated through.

Sauce

Melt the butter in a saucepan and stir in the flour. Cook for several minutes, stirring constantly. Add the stock, milk, sherry, Parmesan cheese and Swiss cheese. Cook until the sauce thickens and the cheeses melt, stirring constantly. Keep warm.

Assembly

Preheat the oven to 350 degrees. Spoon the filling onto the crepes and roll to enclose the filling. Arrange in a buttered ovenproof serving dish. Spoon about half the sauce over the filled crepes. Bake for 30 to 45 minutes or until bubbly and light brown. Serve immediately with the remaining sauce.

The Ramos House Café's Crab Hash

Serves 6

1 pound Dungeness crab meat
1 pound russet potatoes, peeled,
    cooked and mashed
1 bunch scallions, chopped
1/4 cup basil, chopped
1/4 cup mayonnaise
1/4 cup beaten eggs
1/4 cup lemon juice
1 tablespoon dry English mustard
1 teaspoon salt
1 teaspoon black pepper
Pinch of cayenne pepper
Bread crumbs or panko-style
    bread crumbs
Bacon drippings

Combine the crab meat, potatoes, scallions and basil in a large mixing bowl. Add the mayonnaise, eggs, lemon juice, mustard, salt, black pepper and cayenne pepper and mix well. Add just enough bread crumbs to bind the mixture to the consistency of ground beef. Shape into twelve patties. Roll in bread crumbs, coating evenly. Fry in bacon drippings in a skillet until golden brown on both sides. Serve with deep-fried sweet potato threads and chopped chives on a plate sauced with buttermilk dressing.

Situated in the heart of the Los Rios Historical District in San Juan Capistrano, Ramos House was built in 1881 and now contains the renowned Ramos House Café. Owner/Chef John Q. Humphries lives on-site and prepares everything from scratch, even the ice cream that is turned out back. Contemporary American fare with a southern twist is served for breakfast and lunch from a menu that changes daily to ensure the freshest of in-season specialties.

Green Chile Quiche

Serves 8

1 pound lean ground beef
1 (4-ounce) can chopped green chiles
1/4 cup chopped white onion
1/2 teaspoon salt
Black pepper to taste
1 1/2 cups (6 ounces) shredded
　　Swiss cheese
1 unbaked (10-inch) pie shell
4 eggs
1 1/2 cups heavy cream
Salt to taste
1/4 teaspoon cayenne pepper

Preheat the oven to 425 degrees. Cook the ground beef in a skillet, stirring until brown and crumbly; drain. Add the green chiles and onion and mix well. Season with 1/2 teaspoon salt and black pepper. Layer half the Swiss cheese, the ground beef mixture and the remaining Swiss cheese in the pie shell.

Beat the eggs with the cream in a bowl. Season with salt to taste, black pepper and the cayenne pepper. Pour over the layers in the pie shell. Bake for 15 minutes. Reduce the oven temperature to 325 degrees and bake for 40 minutes longer or until a knife inserted into the center comes out clean. Serve with salsa, guacamole and chips.

Duke's Soufflé

Serves 6 to 8

16 ounces Cheddar cheese, shredded
16 ounces Monterey Jack cheese,
    shredded
2 (4-ounce) cans chopped green chiles
4 egg whites
4 egg yolks
1 (14-ounce) can stewed
    tomatoes, drained

Preheat the oven to 350 degrees. Alternate layers of the Cheddar cheese, Monterey Jack cheese and green chiles in a buttered deep baking dish until all the ingredients are used.

Beat the egg whites in a mixing bowl until stiff peaks form. Beat the egg yolks in a bowl and fold into the egg whites. Pour over the layers in the baking dish.

Bake for 30 minutes. Add the tomatoes and press them down into the layers with a fork. Bake for 30 minutes longer.

This recipe is from Pilar Wayne's Favorite and Fabulous Recipes. Academy Award winner and Hollywood icon John Wayne was one of America's most beloved celebrities. He called Newport Beach home, having moved there in the 1960s, and enjoyed sailing his yacht, The Wild Goose, in Newport Bay. In 1979, after the legendary actor's death, the county renamed the airport John Wayne Airport to honor the late star. His family created the John Wayne Cancer Foundation to advance the fight against cancer and remains a prominent and philanthropic fixture in Orange County.

Egg Strata

Serves 8

6 slices French bread
Butter
1 cup (4 ounces) shredded mild
    Cheddar cheese
1 cup (4 ounces) shredded Monterey
    Jack cheese
1/3 cup chopped cooked bacon or
    cooked sausage
6 eggs
2 cups milk
1 teaspoon dry mustard
1/2 teaspoon salt
1/2 teaspoon pepper
Tabasco sauce to taste

Preheat the oven to 350 degrees. Trim the crusts from the bread. Spread both sides of the bread slices with butter and cut into cubes. Sprinkle half the bread in a greased 9×13-inch baking pan. Sprinkle with half the Cheddar cheese, half the Monterey Jack cheese and the bacon. Top with the remaining cheeses and bread.

Combine the eggs, milk, dry mustard, salt, pepper and Tabasco sauce in a bowl and beat until smooth. Pour over the layers. Bake for 45 minutes or until bubbly. Let stand at room temperature for 5 minutes before serving.

Note: You can prepare this in advance and freeze until time to bake. For variation, add spinach, red bell pepper, and/or black olives.

Puffed Apple Pancake

Serves 6 to 8

6 eggs
1 1/2 cups milk
1 cup all-purpose flour
3 tablespoons granulated sugar
1 to 2 teaspoons vanilla extract
1/4 teaspoon cinnamon
1/2 teaspoon salt
1/2 cup (1 stick) butter
2 mild sweet apples, peeled and
    thinly sliced
Brown sugar to taste

Preheat the oven to 425 degrees. Combine the eggs, milk, flour, granulated sugar, vanilla, cinnamon and salt in a mixing bowl and beat until smooth.

Melt the butter in a 9×13-inch baking dish on the center rack of the oven; do not brown. Layer the apple slices in the dish. Bake for 5 minutes or until the butter is sizzling but not brown.

Remove from the oven and pour the egg mixture over the apples. Sprinkle generously with brown sugar. Bake for 20 to 30 minutes or until the top is crusty and brown and the center is set. Serve warm.

Soused French Toast

Serves 4

1 French baguette
4 eggs
3 tablespoons granulated sugar
2 tablespoons orange liqueur
1 teaspoon vanilla extract
1/2 to 1 cup vegetable oil
Confectioners' sugar to taste
Grated orange zest to taste

Cut the baguette into 1-inch slices. Combine the eggs, granulated sugar, liqueur and vanilla in a shallow dish and beat until smooth. Add the bread slices and let stand until the bread is saturated.

Heat the oil in a sauté pan over medium-high heat. Add the bread slices to the sauté pan and cook until light brown on both sides, watching closely to prevent burning. Drain on paper towels.

Place the French toast on serving plates and sprinkle with confectioners' sugar and orange zest. Serve with maple syrup and orange slices.

Blueberry Coffee Cake

Serves 8

1/2 cup broken pecans
1/3 cup packed light brown sugar
1 tablespoon all-purpose flour
1/2 teaspoon cinnamon
1/2 teaspoon nutmeg
1 tablespoon butter, melted
1 1/2 cups sifted all-purpose flour
3/4 cup granulated sugar
2 teaspoons baking powder
1/2 teaspoon salt
1/2 cup half-and-half
1 egg, beaten
1/4 cup vegetable oil
2 ounces cream cheese, softened
1 cup fresh or frozen blueberries

Preheat the oven to 375 degrees. Combine the pecans, brown sugar, 1 tablespoon flour, the cinnamon and nutmeg in a bowl. Add the butter and mix well.

Mix 1 1/2 cups flour, the granulated sugar, baking powder and salt together. Combine the half-and-half, egg, oil and cream cheese in a bowl and beat until smooth. Add the dry ingredients and mix well.

Spoon the batter into a greased 9×9-inch baking pan. Spread the blueberries evenly over the batter and sprinkle with the pecan mixture. Bake for 30 to 35 minutes or until a wooden pick inserted into the center comes out clean.

English Scones

Makes 8

2 1/2 to 2 3/4 cups all-purpose flour
1/3 cup sugar
1 tablespoon baking powder
1/2 teaspoon salt
3/4 cup milk
1/2 cup (1 stick) butter, softened
1 egg
1 egg yolk
Currents (optional)
1 egg white, beaten
Sugar for sprinkling
Homemade Clotted Cream
       (Note at right)

Preheat the oven to 400 degrees. Mix the 2 1/2 cups flour with 1/3 cup sugar, the baking powder and salt in a bowl. Add the milk, butter, egg, egg yolk and currents and mix well. Knead on a floured surface to form a sticky dough, kneading in up to 1/2 cup additional flour if needed for the desired consistency.

Press the dough into a 6-inch circle on a greased baking sheet. Cut into eight wedges. Brush with the egg white and sprinkle with sugar. Bake for 12 to 15 minutes or until golden brown. Serve with Homemade Clotted Cream.

Note: To make Homemade Clotted Cream, place a coffee filter in a strainer over a bowl. Pour 2 cups heavy cream into the filter and place in the refrigerator to allow the whey to drain through the filter, leaving a ring of clotted cream. Scrape the cream down every 2 hours or until enough of the whey drains out to leave a cream the consistency of cream cheese. Store in the refrigerator.

The Valencia orange was created by a farmer in Santa Ana, who named it after a Spanish city known for its excellent oranges. He sold the Valencia orange to The Irvine Company. This division separated from The Irvine Company and became Sunkist.

Pumpkin Muffins

Makes 18 to 24

Pumpkin Muffins

3$\frac{1}{2}$ cups all-purpose flour

2 teaspoons baking soda

1 teaspoon baking powder

1 teaspoon ground cloves

1 teaspoon cinnamon

1 teaspoon nutmeg

$\frac{1}{2}$ teaspoon salt

2 cups canned pumpkin

3 cups sugar

3 eggs

1 cup vegetable oil

1$\frac{1}{2}$ cups chopped walnuts

Orange Glaze

3 cups confectioners' sugar

$\frac{1}{4}$ cup orange juice

2 teaspoons grated orange zest

Muffins

Preheat the oven to 350 degrees. Mix the flour, baking soda, baking powder, cloves, cinnamon, nutmeg and salt in a medium bowl. Combine the pumpkin, sugar, eggs and oil in a mixing bowl and beat until smooth. Add the dry ingredients and mix well. Stir in the walnuts.

Spoon the batter into greased muffin cups. Bake for 20 to 23 minutes or until a wooden pick inserted into the center comes out clean. Cool in the muffin pans for 15 minutes and remove to a wire rack to cool completely.

Glaze

Combine the confectioners' sugar, orange juice and orange zest in a small bowl; stir to mix well. Place waxed paper under the muffins on the wire rack. Spoon the glaze over the cooled muffins, letting the excess run down the sides. Garnish with additional walnuts before the glaze becomes firm.

Goat Cheese Popovers

Makes 12

4 ounces herbed goat cheese
6 eggs
1 1/2 cups all-purpose flour
1 teaspoon dried thyme
Pinch of nutmeg
1 teaspoon salt
1/2 teaspoon freshly ground pepper
2 cups milk
1/2 cup heavy cream
Walnut oil

Preheat the oven to 400 degrees. Cut the goat cheese into eighteen to twenty small pieces. Combine the eggs, flour, thyme, nutmeg, salt and pepper in a blender and pulse to mix well. Add the milk and cream gradually, processing constantly until smooth.

Spray a popover or muffin pan with walnut oil. Warm the pan slightly in the oven. Spoon the batter into the cups, filling halfway. Place one or two pieces of the cheese in the center of each cup. Add enough batter to fill the cups two-thirds full. Bake for 30 to 40 minutes or until puffed and golden brown. Serve warm.

Note: For variety, omit the thyme and substitute your favorite jam or rich dark chocolate for the goat cheese in this recipe.

Banana Bread

Serves 12

1 1/2 cups all-purpose flour
1 teaspoon baking soda
1/2 teaspoon salt
3 ripe bananas, mashed
2 eggs
1 cup sugar
1/4 cup (1/2 stick) butter, melted
1 teaspoon vanilla extract

Preheat the oven to 325 degrees. Mix the flour with the baking soda and salt in a small bowl. Combine the bananas, eggs, sugar, butter and vanilla in a large mixing bowl and mix well. Stir in the dry ingredients just until moistened.

Spoon the batter into a greased and floured 8-inch loaf pan. Bake for 1 hour. Cool in the pan for several minutes and remove to a wire rack to cool completely.

Note: You can substitute whole wheat flour for a portion of the all-purpose flour.

Hawaiian Sweet Bread

Serves 8

1/2 cup milk
1/2 cup pineapple juice
1/3 cup butter
1/3 cup honey
4 1/2 teaspoons dry yeast
2 cups all-purpose flour
1 teaspoon salt
1 egg, beaten
1 drop of yellow food coloring
2 cups all-purpose flour
1 egg
1 tablespoon water

Combine the milk, pineapple juice, butter and honey in a microwave-safe bowl. Microwave on High for 1 minute or to 120 to 130 degrees; the butter may not be completely melted. Mix well.

Mix the yeast with 2 cups flour and the salt in a bowl. Add the heated milk mixture, the beaten egg and the food coloring. Beat with a hand mixer at low speed until moistened. Beat at medium speed for 3 minutes longer.

Stir in 2 cups flour with a large metal spoon. Knead on a floured surface for 5 minutes or until smooth and elastic. Place in a greased bowl, turning to coat the surface. Let rise, covered with plastic wrap, out of the direct sun for 1 to 1 1/2 hours or until doubled in bulk.

Punch down the dough and shape into a round loaf. Place in a greased 9-inch baking pan. Let rise, covered, for 15 to 20 minutes longer.

Preheat the oven to 350 degrees. Mix one egg with the water in a small bowl. Brush over the loaf. Bake for 35 to 40 minutes or until golden brown.

Zucchini Bread

Makes 2 loaves

3 eggs
2 cups sugar
1 cup vegetable oil
3 zucchini, grated
2 cups all-purpose flour
1 cup chopped nuts
1 teaspoon baking powder
2 teaspoons cinnamon
2 teapoons vanilla extract
1 teaspoon salt

Preheat the oven to 350 degrees. Combine the eggs, sugar and oil in a mixing bowl and beat until smooth. Add the zucchini, flour and nuts and mix well. Stir in the baking powder, cinnamon, vanilla and salt.

Spoon into two greased loaf pans. Bake for 1 hour. Let cool in the pans for several minutes and remove to a wire rack to cool completely.

Bacon-Wrapped Bread Sticks

Serves 10 or more

16 ounces sliced bacon
1/4 cup (or more) grated
    Parmesan cheese
1/4 cup (or more) packed brown sugar
1 package bread sticks

Preheat the oven to 400 degrees. Slice the bacon into halves or thirds. Mix 1/4 cup Parmesan cheese with 1/4 cup brown sugar in a shallow bowl. Increase the amount of the mixture as needed, adding equal parts of the cheese and brown sugar.

Wrap one piece of the bacon spirally around each bread stick, leaving the desired portion of bread stick at the end as a small handle. Coat the bacon with the brown sugar mixture.

Arrange the bread sticks on a rack in a baking pan. Bake until the bacon is crisp, watching carefully to prevent burning and turning once during the baking process.

Note: You can cover the unwrapped portion of the bread stick with foil to help prevent burning. Bake the bread sticks as soon as they are wrapped to keep them from becoming soggy.

Garlic Artichoke Bread

Serves 8

1 (6-ounce) jar marinated artichokes
1 (16-ounce) package frozen white bread
    dough, thawed
1 cup (4 ounces) grated Parmesan cheese
4 garlic cloves, minced or crushed
2 teaspoons dried basil
2 teaspoons dried oregano
1/4 cup (1 ounce) grated Parmesan cheese

Preheat the oven to 375 degrees. Drain the artichokes, reserving the artichokes and the marinade separately; chop the artichokes.

Roll the dough into a 12×18-inch rectangle on a floured surface. Let rest for 5 minutes if the dough is springy. Brush half the reserved marinade over the dough. Sprinkle with the artichokes, 1 cup Parmesan cheese, the garlic, basil and oregano. Roll tightly from a wide side to enclose the filling.

Shape into a ring on a greased 12×15-inch baking sheet; pinch the ends to seal. Brush with the remaining marinade. Cover lightly with plastic wrap and let stand in a warm place for 30 minutes or until puffy.

Bake for 15 minutes. Sprinkle with 1/4 cup Parmesan cheese. Bake for 10 to 15 minutes longer or until golden brown. Remove to a wire rack to cool or serve immediately. Store in an airtight container in the refrigerator for up to 2 days or in the freezer for longer. Serve as an appetizer or as an accompaniment to a salad dinner.

Fruit, Berry and Nut Granola

Serves 40

4 cups rolled oats
2 cups shredded coconut
2 cups whole, slivered or
    sliced almonds
2 tablespoons brown sugar
2 tablespoons water
1/3 cup canola oil
1/3 cup clover honey
1 teaspoon almond extract
1 teaspoon vanilla extract
2 teaspoons cinnamon
3 tablespoons flaxseed meal
1 cup shredded coconut
1 cup roasted unsalted cashews
1 cup dried cherries
1 cup dried blueberries
1 cup dried cranberries
1 cup dried strawberries

Toss the oats, 2 cups coconut and the almonds in a large bowl to mix well. Blend the brown sugar with the water in a small bowl. Whisk in the canola oil, honey, almond extract and vanilla. Pour over the oats mixture and mix well. Sprinkle with the cinnamon and flaxseed meal and stir to mix well.

Spread the oats mixture in a 13×18-inch baking pan. Bake for 15 to 30 minutes or until golden brown, stirring every 5 minutes. Let stand until cool, stirring occasionally. Stir in 1 cup coconut, the cashews, cherries, blueberries, cranberries and strawberries. Store in an airtight container or sealable plastic bags. Serve as a snack, in a parfait with fresh berries and vanilla yogurt or use as a gift.

Note: You can substitute any combination of dried fruit that you prefer, such as figs, sour cherries, or thinly sliced apricots.

The Good Life

SWEETS

*I*n Orange County, we know how to live the good life, which makes us a popular tourist destination. Miles of beautiful beaches, glorious mountain ranges, and perfect weather almost everyday are what get the people here. It's the shopping and dining that keep them coming back for more.

Two of Orange Counties' premier shopping destinations are South Coast Plaza and Fashion Island. Part 5th Avenue, part Michigan Avenue, South Coast Plaza hosts more than 280 boutiques from the most popular ready-to-wear labels to the most exclusive haute couture. Fashion Island is Southern California's premier, open-air retail center, combining coastal luxury shopping, entertainment, and fine dining. With the biggest names, the hottest fashions, and some of the most unique boutiques, shops, and stores in the world, Orange County knows how to live the high life, which has earned us quite the reputation. That reputation has made its way into pop culture thanks in part to recent popular television shows that highlight the wealthy lifestyle that exists here.

What began as farm country full of orange groves and grape vines, has been elevated to the stuff of prime-time dreams, full of beautiful ocean-front homes, chic boutiques, and sexy citizens. What's the real Orange County? Well, a little bit of both.

Pumpkin Bread Pudding with Caramel Sauce

Serves 10

Pumpkin Bread Pudding

1 (15-ounce) can pumpkin
2 eggs
1 cup packed dark brown sugar
1/2 cup half-and-half
1 1/2 teaspoons pumpkin pie spice
1 1/2 teaspoons cinnamon
1 1/2 teaspoons vanilla extract
10 cups (1/2-inch) egg bread cubes
1/2 cup golden raisins (optional)
Confectioners' sugar

Caramel Sauce

1 1/4 cups packed dark brown sugar
1/2 cup (1 stick) unsalted butter
1/2 cup heavy cream

Pudding

Combine the pumpkin, eggs, brown sugar, half-and-half, pumpkin pie spice, cinnamon and vanilla in a large bowl and whisk to mix well. Fold in the bread cubes. Stir in the raisins. Spoon the mixture into a greased 7×11-inch baking dish. Let stand for 15 minutes.

Preheat the oven to 350 degrees. Bake for 40 minutes or until a tester inserted into the center comes out clean. Sift confectioners' sugar over the top. Serve warm with the caramel sauce.

Sauce

Combine the brown sugar and butter in a heavy medium saucepan. Cook over medium heat until the butter melts, whisking to blend well. Whisk in the cream. Cook for 3 minutes or until the brown sugar dissolves completely and the sauce is smooth, whisking constantly. Serve with the bread pudding.

In 1906 the Knott family moved to Buena Park to grow berries. Mrs. Knott eventually opened a small restaurant in her home, serving fried chicken dinners on her wedding china to travelers between Los Angeles and San Diego. Walter Knott began Knott's Berry Farm amusements and attractions as a way to keep customers entertained while they waited to be seated at the restaurant.

Chocolate Almond Cheesecake

Serves 12

Chocolate Crust
1 1/2 cups chocolate cookie crumbs
1/4 cup plus 1 teaspoon sugar

Cheesecake Filling
24 ounces cream cheese, softened
1 cup sugar
4 eggs
1/3 cup heavy cream
1/4 cup amaretto
1 teaspoon vanilla extract

Sour Cream Topping
2 cups sour cream
1 tablespoon sugar
1 teaspoon vanilla extract

Crust
Combine the cookie crumbs with the sugar in a bowl and mix well. Press over the bottom and side of a buttered 9 1/2-inch springform pan. Place in the freezer.

Filling
Preheat the oven to 375 degrees. Combine the cream cheese and sugar in a mixing bowl and beat until fluffy. Beat in the eggs one at a time. Add the cream, amaretto and vanilla and beat until light. Bake for 1 hour or until the center is set. Let stand for 5 minutes.

Topping
Combine the sour cream, sugar and vanilla in a bowl and mix until smooth. Spread over the cheesecake. Let stand until completely cool. Cover lightly and chill in the refrigerator for 8 hours or longer.

Place the cheesecake on a serving plate and remove the side of the springform pan. Garnish with chocolate cookie crumbs or chocolate shavings.

Oreo Ice Cream Cake

Serves 16

24 chocolate sandwich cookies, crushed
1/4 cup (1/2 stick) butter, softened
1/2 gallon vanilla ice cream, softened
1 1/2 cups Spanish peanuts
1 cup (6 ounces) chocolate chips
1/2 cup (1 stick) butter
2 cups confectioners' sugar
1 (13-ounce) can evaporated milk
12 ounces whipped topping

Combine the cookie crumbs and 1/4 cup butter in a bowl and mix well. Press over the bottom of a freezer-safe 9×13-inch dish. Spread the ice cream over the cookie layer and sprinkle with the peanuts. Freeze until firm.

Combine the chocolate chips, 1/2 cup butter, the confectioners' sugar and evaporated milk in a saucepan. Bring to a boil and cook for 8 minutes, stirring frequently. Cool completely. Spread over the ice cream layer and top with the whipped topping.

Freeze until firm or for up to 1 month. Let stand at room temperature for 15 to 20 minutes before serving.

Spumoni Charlotte

Serves 10

20 ladyfingers, split
1/4 cup amaretto
2/3 cup chocolate wafer crumbs
1 quart vanilla ice cream, softened
1 tablespoon rum
1 (6-ounce) jar maraschino
    cherries, drained
1 quart pistachio ice cream, softened
1 cup heavy whipping cream
1/2 cup sifted confectioners' sugar
1 tablespoon rum

Brush the cut sides of the ladyfingers with the amaretto. Coat lightly with the chocolate wafer crumbs. Arrange over the bottom and side of a 9-inch springform pan.

Combine the vanilla ice cream and 1 tablespoon rum in a bowl and mix well. Spoon into the prepared pan, spreading evenly to the edge. Arrange the maraschino cherries over the top and press lightly into the ice cream. Spread the pistachio ice cream evenly over the top. Freeze for 8 hours or longer.

Combine the whipping cream, confectioners' sugar and rum in a mixing bowl and beat until soft peaks form. Spread over the frozen layers. Freeze until firm.

To serve, let the charlotte stand at room temperature for 10 minutes. Place on a serving plate and remove the side of the springform pan. Garnish with a maraschino cherry in the center and additional cookie crumbs.

Latvian Apple Dessert

Serves 8 to 10

1 cup (2 sticks) butter, softened
8 ounces cream cheese, softened
2 cups all-purpose flour
3 pounds Granny Smith apples,
    peeled and cut into medium slices
Granulated sugar to taste
2 tablespoons brown sugar
Cinnamon to taste
2 tablespoons cornstarch
1 egg, beaten

Combine the butter with the cream cheese in a bowl and beat until creamy. Add the flour and mix well to form a dough. Chill, covered, for 3 hours.

Preheat the oven to 450 degrees. Cut two pieces of waxed paper 1 inch bigger than a 9×13-inch baking dish. Grease the bottom and sides of the dish. Place the pieces of waxed paper on two paper towels on a work surface and dust with flour.

Divide the chilled dough into two portions, making one portion slightly larger than the other. Press and then roll the larger portion into a 9×13-inch rectangle on one piece of the waxed paper. Trim to fit the dish if necessary. Invert the dough with the waxed paper in the prepared baking dish and remove the waxed paper.

Layer half the apples over the dough. Sprinkle with granulated sugar. Layer with the remaining apples. Sprinkle with granulated sugar, the brown sugar, cinnamon and cornstarch. Fill in spaces with apples cut to fit.

Roll the remaining dough on the remaining piece of waxed paper to fit the baking dish. Use the waxed paper to invert it over the apples; seal to the edges of the dish. Cut slashes in the dough to vent. Brush with the beaten egg.

Bake for 1 hour or until the apples are tender, checking every 20 minutes with a wooden pick. Serve warm or cold.

The Ramos House Café's Warm Banana and Berry Shortcakes

Serves 6 to 8

Biscuits

5 cups all-purpose flour

1/4 cup sugar

1/4 cup baking powder

1 teaspoon salt

3/4 cup (1 1/2 sticks) butter, chilled and
     cut into 1/2-inch pieces

1 1/4 cups (2 sticks) margarine, chilled and
     cut into 1/2-inch pieces

1 1/2 cups buttermilk

Fruit Filling

4 bananas, sliced

2 tablespoons butter

3/4 cup sugar

3 cups mixed blueberries, blackberries
     and raspberries

2 cups sweetened whipped cream

Biscuits

Sift the flour, sugar, baking powder and salt into a bowl. Work the butter into the flour mixture by hand or with a pastry blender until the mixture forms crumbs the size of large peas. Add the margarine in the same manner. Add the buttermilk and mix just until combined; do not overmix.

Roll the dough 2 inches thick on a floured surface. Cut with a biscuit cutter and arrange on a baking sheet. Cover with plastic wrap and freeze for 2 hours or longer.

Preheat the oven to 375 degrees. Bake the biscuits on the upper oven rack for 25 minutes or until golden brown.

Filling

Sauté the bananas in the butter in a sauté pan until golden brown. Add the sugar and cook until the sugar dissolves and begins to caramelize, stirring constantly. Add the berries and sauté for 30 seconds.

Split six to eight biscuits and place the bottom halves on serving plates. Spoon the hot fruit filling over the biscuits and top with the whipped cream and biscuit tops. Garnish with confectioners' sugar and serve warm.

Note: The leftover biscuits are wonderful for breakfast the next morning.

Italian Parfait with Mascarpone, Amaretto and Fresh Berries

Serves 6

8 ounces mascarpone cheese
3 tablespoons amaretto
3 tablespoons heavy cream
2 tablespoons sugar
3 cups mixed sliced strawberries,
    raspberries, blueberries
    and blackberries
3 tablespoons amaretto
1 tablespoon sugar
2 1/2 cups amaretti crumbs
Additional amaretto

Combine the mascarpone cheese, 3 tablespoons amaretto, the cream and 2 tablespoons sugar in a medium bowl and mix gently to dissolve the sugar. Chill, covered, for 30 minutes.

Combine the berries with 3 tablespoons amaretto and 1 tablespoon sugar in a medium bowl. Toss to coat the berries well. Chill, covered, for 30 minutes.

Spoon 2 tablespoons of the cookie crumbs into each of six goblets. Sprinkle lightly with additional amaretto. Spoon the berries and any accumulated juices into the goblets. Top with the mascarpone cheese mixture and the remaining cookie crumbs. Cover and chill for 30 minutes to 2 hours.

Pots de Crème

Serves 4 or 5

1 cup (6 ounces) gourmet semisweet
    chocolate chips
1 egg
3/4 cup half-and-half

Combine the chocolate chips and egg in a blender. Bring the half-and-half just to a boil in a saucepan. Add to the blender and process for 1 minute. Pour into four or five pot de crème cups or ramekins. Chill for 6 hours. Serve with whipped cream.

Note: The hot half-and-half added to the egg should be sufficient to cook it, but if you are concerned about using uncooked eggs, use eggs pasteurized in their shells, which are sold in some specialty food stores, or use an equivalent amount of pasteurized egg substitute.

K'ya's Chocolate Soufflés

Serves 4

Butter for coating
Superfine sugar for sprinkling
6 ounces bittersweet chocolate, chopped
2/3 cup unsalted butter, chopped
4 egg yolks
4 egg whites
1/4 teaspoon cream of tartar
3 tablespoons superfine sugar
Confectioners' sugar

Preheat the oven to 425 degrees. Butter four 6-ounce ramekins generously and sprinkle with superfine sugar; tap out any excess sugar. Arrange on a baking sheet.

Melt the chocolate with 2/3 cup butter in a heavy saucepan over low heat, stirring until smooth. Cool slightly. Add the egg yolks and beat to mix well. Let cool to room temperature, stirring occasionally.

Whisk the egg whites in a clean grease-free bowl until frothy. Add the cream of tartar and whisk briskly until soft peaks form. Sprinkle with 3 tablespoons superfine sugar, 1 tablespoon at a time, whisking constantly until the peaks are stiff and glossy.

Stir one-third of the egg whites into the cooled chocolate, then add the chocolate mixture to the egg whites. Fold in with a rubber spatula, cutting down to the bottom of the bowl then along the side and up to the top in a semicircular motion to combine; some white streaks will remain.

Spoon into the prepared ramekins. Bake for 10 to 12 minutes or until the soufflés are set at the edges, but the centers shake slightly. Sprinkle with confectioners' sugar and serve immediately with ice cream.

Nestled inside the trendy Hotel Menage in Anaheim and the beautiful Hotel La Casa del Camino in Laguna Beach, K'ya Restaurant & Bar melds cosmopolitan and coastal motifs to create a casual, romantic decor and a thoroughly inviting place to dine. The spirit of diversity is well represented both in the kitchen and in the menu, which offers sensational dishes influenced by the flavors of the Pacific Rim, Europe, the Mediterranean, and local friends.

Tiramisu

Serves 6

3 egg yolks
3 tablespoons sugar
$1/3$ cup coffee liqueur
1 egg white
$1/4$ cup very strong espresso or
    strong coffee
8 ounces mascarpone cheese,
    at room temperature
1 cup plus 2 tablespoons heavy
    whipping cream
4 ounces ladyfingers
$1/2$ cup coffee liqueur

Cook the egg yolks and sugar in a double boiler over simmering water until ivory in color, beating constantly. Add $1/3$ cup liqueur and cook until thickened, whisking constantly. Cool to room temperature.

Beat the egg white in a mixing bowl until stiff peaks form. Fold into the cooled egg yolk mixture to form a zabaglione. Blend the espresso into the mascarpone cheese in a bowl. Beat the whipping cream in a bowl until soft peaks form.

Dip the ladyfingers in $1/2$ cup liqueur. Arrange in a single layer in a 9-inch dish. Layer half the mascarpone mixture, half the zabaglione and half the whipped cream in the prepared dish. Repeat the layers, beginning with the mascarpone mixture, and garnish with shaved chocolate. Chill for several hours before serving.

Pineapple Kabobs with Green Lemon Syrup

Serves 8

Green Lemon Syrup
Juice of 1 green (unripe) lemon or lime
5 tablespoons brown sugar

Syrup
Combine the lemon juice and brown sugar in a small saucepan. Bring to a boil and cook until the brown sugar dissolves, stirring to mix well.

Pineapple Kabobs
$3/4$ cup heavy cream
2 tablespoons sugar
2 tablespoons canned coconut milk
1 pineapple

Kabobs
Soak eight bamboo skewers in water for 30 minutes or longer. Combine the cream and sugar in a mixing bowl and beat until thickened. Add the coconut milk gradually, beating constantly. Preheat the grill or oven to high. Core and slice the pineapple; cut the slices into bite-size pieces. Thread onto the bamboo skewers. Drizzle with the syrup. Grill or bake the kabobs until the pineapple appears caramelized. Serve with the coconut cream and remaining syrup.

Dutch Apple Pie

Serves 6 to 8

1 cup all-purpose flour
1/2 cup packed brown sugar
1/2 cup (1 stick) butter, chilled and
    chopped
1 cup granulated sugar
1/3 cup all-purpose flour
1 teaspoon nutmeg
1 teaspoon cinnamon
Pinch of salt
8 cups thinly sliced Jonathan apples or
    McIntosh apples
1 unbaked pie shell

Mix 1/2 cup flour and the brown sugar in a bowl. Cut in the butter with a pastry cutter until crumbly.

Preheat the oven to 400 degrees. Combine the granulated sugar, 1/3 cup flour, the nutmeg, cinnamon and salt in a large bowl. Add the apples and toss to coat evenly. Arrange the apples in the pie shell. Sprinkle with the topping; the filling will be mounded, but will bake down.

Bake for 40 minutes. Place foil over the pie to prevent overbrowning if necessary and bake for 10 minutes longer.

Pecan Chocolate Pie

Serves 6 to 8

1 1/2 cups pecan halves
1 cup (6 ounces) semisweet
    chocolate chips
1 unbaked (9-inch) pie shell
4 eggs, beaten
1 cup corn syrup
1/2 cup granulated sugar
1/2 cup packed light brown sugar
1 teaspoon vanilla extract
Pinch of salt

Preheat the oven to 375 degrees. Sprinkle the pecans and chocolate chips evenly in the pie shell. Combine the eggs, corn syrup, granulated sugar, brown sugar, vanilla and salt in a bowl and whisk until smooth.

Pour the egg mixture into the prepared pie shell. Bake for 50 to 60 minutes or until set. Cool slightly before serving. Serve with warm caramel sauce, confectioners' sugar or vanilla ice cream.

Key Lime Pie

Serves 6 to 8

5 eggs
5 egg yolks
2 (14-ounce) cans sweetened
  condensed milk
1 cup freshly squeezed Key lime juice or
  lime juice
1 graham cracker pie shell

Beat the eggs and egg yolks in a bowl. Add the sweetened condensed milk and lime juice and mix well. Spoon into the pie shell. Freeze until firm. Garnish each serving with sweetened whipped cream, a fresh mint leaf and a very thin slice of lime rolled cornucopia style.

Note: If you are concerned about using uncooked eggs, use eggs pasteurized in their shells, which are sold in some specialty food stores, or use an equivalent amount of pasteurized egg substitute.

Black Russian Bundt Cake

Serves 12

Black Russian Bundt Cake
1 (2-layer) package yellow cake mix
1 (4-ounce) package chocolate
  instant pudding mix
1 cup vegetable oil
4 eggs
1/4 cup vodka
1/2 cup coffee liqueur
1/2 cup water

Cake
Preheat the oven to 350 degrees. Combine the cake mix, pudding mix, oil, eggs, vodka, liqueur and water in a mixing bowl. Beat for 4 minutes.
Spoon the batter into a greased and floured bundt pan. Bake for 50 minutes. Cool in the pan for 15 to 30 minutes. Remove to a wire rack to cool completely.

Black Russian Glaze
2 tablespoons melted butter
1/2 cup (or more) confectioners' sugar
1 tablespoon coffee liqueur
1 teaspoon vodka
1/2 teaspoon vanilla extract

Glaze
Combine the butter, confectioners' sugar, liqueur, vodka and vanilla in a mixing bowl and whisk until smooth; whisk in additional confectioners' sugar if needed for the desired consistency. Drizzle over the cooled cake.

Brown Sugar Oatmeal Cake

Serves 12

Brown Sugar Oatmeal Cake

1 1/4 cups boiling water

1 cup quick-cooking oats

1 1/2 cups sifted all-purpose flour

1 teaspoon baking soda

3/4 teaspoon cinnamon

1/2 teaspoon salt

1/2 cup (1 stick) butter, softened

1 cup granulated sugar

1 cup packed brown sugar

2 eggs

1 teaspoon vanilla extract

Coconut Pecan Frosting

3/4 cup shredded coconut

1 cup packed brown sugar

1/2 cup chopped pecans

1/3 cup butter, melted

3 tablespoons half-and-half or
   nonfat milk

1 teaspoon vanilla extract

Cake

Pour the boiling water over the oats in a bowl; cover with plastic wrap and let stand for 20 minutes. Sift the flour with the baking soda, cinnamon and salt.

Preheat the oven to 350 degrees. Cream the butter in a mixing bowl. Add the granulated sugar and brown sugar gradually, beating constantly until fluffy. Beat in the eggs and vanilla. Stir in the oats. Add the dry ingredients and mix well.

Spoon into a greased and floured 9×13-inch baking pan. Bake for 35 minutes. Cool on a wire rack.

Frosting

Preheat the broiler. Combine the coconut, brown sugar, pecans, butter, half-and-half and vanilla in an ovenproof bowl and mix well. Broil for 5 minutes or until bubbly, watching carefully to prevent burning. Spread over the cake.

Note: You may also make a 2-layer cake if desired. Spoon the batter into two round cake pans and bake for 27 minutes.

The Ultimate Carrot Cake

Serves 12

Carrot Cake

2 cups all-purpose flour

2 teaspoons baking soda

2 teaspoons cinnamon

1 teaspoon salt

1 pound carrots, shredded

1 cup golden raisins (optional)

1 (8-ounce) can crushed
     pineapple, drained

1 cup chopped walnuts

1 tablespoon all-purpose flour

2 cups sugar

1^1/$_3$ cups vegetable oil

3 eggs, at room temperature

1 cup sour cream

1 teaspoon vanilla extract

Cream Cheese Frosting

12 ounces cream cheese, softened

1 cup (2 sticks) unsalted butter, softened

1 teaspoon vanilla extract

1 (1-pound) package confectioners' sugar

Cake

Preheat the oven to 350 degrees. Sift 2 cups flour with the baking soda, cinnamon and salt. Combine the carrots, raisins, pineapple, walnuts and 1 tablespoon flour in a bowl and toss to mix well.

Combine the sugar, oil, eggs and sour cream in a large mixing bowl and beat until pale yellow in color. Beat in the vanilla. Add the dry ingredients and beat to mix well. Stir in the carrot mixture.

Spoon the batter into a bundt pan sprayed with nonstick cooking spray. Bake for 45 to 50 minutes or until the cake tests done. Remove to a wire rack to cool completely.

Frosting

Combine the cream cheese, butter and vanilla in a mixing bowl and beat until light and fluffy. Add the confectioners' sugar and beat until smooth. Spread over the cooled cake.

Milk Chocolate Brownie Cake

Serves 12

Milk Chocolate Brownie Cake

2 cups all-purpose flour

2 cups sugar

1 teaspoon baking soda

1/2 teaspoon salt

1 cup (2 sticks) butter

1 cup water

1/3 cup baking cocoa

1/2 cup buttermilk

2 eggs

Milk Chocolate Frosting

1/2 cup (1 stick) butter

1/3 cup baking cocoa

1/3 cup milk

Pinch of salt

1 (1-pound) package confectioners' sugar

Cake

Preheat the oven to 375 degrees. Mix the flour, sugar, baking soda and salt in a large bowl. Melt the butter in a small saucepan over medium heat. Add the water and baking cocoa and mix to blend well. Add to the dry ingredients and mix well. Stir in the buttermilk and eggs gradually.

Spoon the batter into a lightly greased and floured 9×13-inch baking pan. Bake for 20 to 25 minutes or until a wooden pick inserted into the center comes out clean. Cool on a wire rack.

Frosting

Melt the butter in a saucepan over low heat. Stir in the baking cocoa, milk and salt. Pour into a mixing bowl and beat with a hand mixer until smooth. Add the confectioners' sugar gradually, beating constantly until incorporated. Spread over the cooled cake. Let stand until the frosting is firm before serving.

Note: You can prepare this recipe in round 8- or 9-inch cake pans, reducing the baking time as needed.

Orange Marmalade Cake

Serves 8 to 10

Orange Marmalade Cake

1 (2-layer) package yellow cake mix
1 (4-ounce) package vanilla instant
    pudding mix
1 1/3 cups orange juice
3 eggs
1/2 cup vegetable oil
1 tablespoon grated orange zest
1 teaspoon vanilla extract

Orange Syrup

3/4 cup orange juice
2 tablespoons sugar

Fluffy Frosting

3/4 cup heavy whipping cream
3 tablespoons sugar
3/4 cup sour cream

Assembly

1 cup orange marmalade

Cake

Preheat the oven to 350 degrees. Beat the cake mix, pudding mix, orange juice, eggs, oil, orange zest and vanilla in a mixing bowl at low speed until moistened. Beat at medium speed until well combined.

Spoon into two 9-inch cake pans sprayed with nonstick cooking spray and floured; smooth the tops. Bake on the same oven rack for 25 to 30 minutes or until the tops spring back when lightly pressed.

Cool the layers in the pans on a wire rack for 5 minutes. Loosen from the sides of the pans with a sharp knife and remove, right side up, to the wire rack. Cool for 20 minutes.

Syrup

Combine the orange juice with the sugar in a small bowl and whisk until the sugar dissolves. Poke holes in the tops of the cake layers and drizzle the syrup gradually over the layers. Cool for 30 minutes or to room temperature.

Frosting

Chill a large mixing bowl and beaters. Beat the whipping cream in the chilled bowl at high speed until soft peaks form. Add the sugar gradually, beating until stiff peaks form. Fold in the sour cream.

Assembly

Heat the orange marmalade in a small saucepan until melted to spreading consistency. Place one cake layer on a cake plate. Spread two-thirds of the marmalade over the top. Top with the second cake layer. Spoon the remaining marmalade into the center and spread to within 1/4 inch of the edge. Spread the frosting over the side and top border of the cake, leaving the marmalade unfrosted. Store in the refrigerator.

Note: Make the cake in advance to allow the flavors to develop.

Pumpkin Cake

Serves 24

Pumpkin Cake

4 eggs
2 cups sugar
1 cup vegetable oil
1 (15-ounce) can pumpkin
2 cups all-purpose flour
2 tablespoons baking powder
1 teaspoon baking soda
2 teaspoons cinnamon
1/2 teaspoon ginger
1/2 teaspoon ground cloves
1/2 teaspoon nutmeg
1/2 teaspoon salt

Creamy Frosting

6 ounces cream cheese, softened
1 tablespoon heavy cream
6 tablespoons butter, softened
1 teaspoon vanilla extract
4 cups confectioners' sugar

Cake

Preheat the oven to 350 degrees. Combine the eggs, sugar, oil and pumpkin in a mixing bowl and beat until smooth. Add the flour, baking powder, baking soda, cinnamon, ginger, cloves, nutmeg and salt and mix well.

Spoon the batter into a greased and floured 12×15-inch baking pan. Bake for 25 minutes or until the cake tests done. Cool on a wire rack for 2 hours.

Frosting

Combine the cream cheese, cream, butter and vanilla in a mixing bowl and mix well. Add the confectioners' sugar and beat until smooth. Spread over the cooled cake.

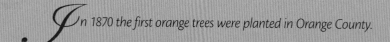
In 1870 the first orange trees were planted in Orange County.

Rum Bundt Cake

Serves 8

Rum Bundt Cake

1/2 cup chopped pecans
1 (2-layer) package yellow cake mix
1 (4-ounce) package vanilla instant
    pudding mix
1/2 cup light rum
1/2 cup water
1/2 cup vegetable oil
4 eggs

Rum Glaze

1 1/2 cups sugar
3/4 cup (1 1/2 sticks) butter
1/4 cup light rum
1/4 cup water

Cake

Preheat the oven to 350 degrees. Sprinkle the pecans into a greased and floured bundt pan.

Combine the cake mix and pudding mix in a medium bowl and mix well. Combine the rum, water, oil and eggs in a large mixing bowl and mix well. Add the cake and pudding mixes and beat for 2 minutes or until smooth and creamy.

Spoon the batter into the prepared bundt pan. Bake for 50 minutes or until a wooden pick inserted into the center comes out clean.

Glaze

Combine the sugar, butter, rum and water in a saucepan about 10 minutes before the cake is done. Bring to a boil and cook for 5 minutes, stirring to dissolve the sugar completely.

Pour over the hot cake, easing the cake away from the side of the bundt pan to allow the glaze to coat the side.

Cool the cake in the pan for just 1 hour. Invert onto a serving plate and scrape any glaze remaining in the pan onto the cake. Serve warm or cool with whipped cream, ice cream or mixed fresh berries dusted with confectioners' sugar and drizzled with Grand Marnier.

Note: Do not allow the cake to remaining in the pan longer than one hour to prevent the glaze from sticking to the pan and making removal of the cake difficult.

Vanilla Bean Pound Cake

Serves 10

2½ cups plus 3 tablespoons
    unbleached flour
1 tablespoon potato starch
1½ teaspoons vanilla powder
¼ teaspoon baking soda
½ teaspoon salt
1 cup sour cream
2 tablespoons heavy cream
¼ cup brandy
1 tablespoon amaretto
1 tablespoon rum
1½ teaspoons whiskey
1½ teaspoons vanilla extract
1 cup (2 sticks) unsalted butter
3 cups extra-fine sugar
1 vanilla bean (optional)
5 eggs
1 egg yolk

Preheat the oven to 350 degrees. Whisk the flour with the potato starch, vanilla powder, baking soda and salt in a large bowl. Combine the sour cream, heavy cream, brandy, amaretto, rum, whiskey and vanilla in a large bowl and whisk gently to mix well.

Combine the butter and sugar in a large mixing bowl. Scrape the seeds from the vanilla bean into the bowl; discard the pod. Mix at low speed for 2 to 3 minutes. Beat in the eggs and egg yolk one at a time. Add the dry ingredients and sour cream mixture alternately, mixing for just 1 minute. Scrape down the side of the bowl and mix for 15 to 20 seconds longer or until smooth.

Spoon the batter into a bundt pan sprayed with nonstick cooking spray, filling three-fourths full. Reserve any remaining batter for cupcakes. Smooth the top with a rubber spatula. Bake on the center oven rack for 45 minutes or until a wooden tester comes out with just a few crumbs.

Cool the cake in the pan for 5 to 10 minutes. Remove to a plate to cool completely. Garnish each serving with confectioners' sugar and serve with whipped cream and berries.

Macadamia White Chocolate Chip Cookies

Makes 3 dozen

1¹/₂ cups all-purpose flour
¹/₂ teaspoon baking powder
¹/₂ teaspoon salt
³/₄ cup (1¹/₂ sticks) unsalted
    butter, softened
¹/₂ cup packed brown sugar
¹/₂ cup granulated sugar
1 egg
1 teaspoon vanilla extract
2 tablespoons light corn syrup
2 cups (12 ounces) white chocolate chips
1 cup macadamia halves

Preheat the oven to 350 degrees. Mix the flour, baking powder and salt together. Cream the butter, brown sugar and granulated sugar in a mixing bowl until light and fluffy. Beat in the egg and vanilla. Add the dry ingredients gradually, mixing well with a spoon. Add the corn syrup, white chocolate chips and macadamias and mix well.

Drop by teaspoonfuls 4 inches apart on an ungreased cookie sheet. Bake for 9 to 12 minutes or just until the cookies begin to brown. Cool on the cookie sheet for several minutes; remove to a wire rack to cool completely. Store in an airtight container.

Oatmeal Date Cookies

Makes 3 dozen

¹/₂ cup (1 stick) butter, softened
³/₄ cup packed brown sugar
¹/₄ cup granulated sugar
1 egg
1 cup all-purpose flour
¹/₂ tablespoon baking soda
¹/₄ tablespoon baking powder
1 tablespoon vanilla extract
1 cup cornflakes
1 cup rolled oats
1 cup chopped walnuts
1 (8-ounce) package pitted dates, chopped

Preheat the oven to 350 degrees. Cream the butter with the brown sugar and granulated sugar in a mixing bowl until light and fluffy. Add the egg, flour, baking soda, baking powder and vanilla and mix well. Stir in the cornflakes, oats, walnuts and dates.

Drop by spoonfuls onto a greased cookie sheet. Bake for 10 to 12 minutes. Cool on the cookie sheet for 2 minutes; remove to a wire rack to cool completely.

Oatmeal Cherry Chocolate Cookies

Makes 3 dozen

1¹/₂ cups all-purpose flour
1 teaspoon baking soda
1 teaspoon cinnamon
¹/₂ teaspoon fine sea salt
1 cup (2 sticks) butter, softened
1 cup packed brown sugar
1 cup granulated sugar
2 eggs, at room temperature
1 teaspoon vanilla extract
¹/₂ teaspoon almond extract
2 cups rolled oats
1¹/₂ cups dried tart cherries, chopped
1 cup (6 ounces) miniature chocolate
    chips
¹/₂ cup coarsely chopped dark chocolate

Preheat the oven to 350 degrees. Sift the flour with the baking soda, cinnamon and sea salt. Cream the butter, brown sugar and granulated sugar in a mixing bowl until light and fluffy. Beat in the eggs, vanilla and almond extract. Add the dry ingredients and mix well. Stir in the oats, cherries, chocolate chips and dark chocolate.

Drop onto a cookie sheet with a small ice cream scoop. Bake for 12 to 14 minutes or until golden brown. Cool on the cookie sheet for 1 minute; remove to a wire rack to cool completely.

Chocolate Chip Tea Cookies

Makes 4 dozen

1 cup (2 sticks) butter, softened
¹/₂ cup confectioners' sugar, sifted
1 teaspoon vanilla extract
2 cups all-purpose flour
2 teaspoons cinnamon (optional)
²/₃ cup finely chopped nuts (optional)
2 cups (12 ounces) miniature semisweet
    chocolate chips

Preheat the oven to 350 degrees. Cream the butter and confectioners' sugar in a large mixing bowl until light and fluffy. Beat in the vanilla. Add the flour, cinnamon and nuts gradually, beating constantly. Stir in the chocolate chips.

Shape the dough into 1-inch balls and place on an ungreased cookie sheet. Bake for 10 to 12 minutes or until set and light golden brown on the bottom. Cool on the cookie sheet for 2 minutes; remove to a wire rack to cool completely.

Rebecca Lacko's Ultra-Healthy Brownies with Icing

Serves 12

1 cup walnuts
1 cup dates
1/3 cup baking cocoa
2 avocados, chopped
1/2 cup agave nectar
1/4 cup baking cocoa
1 tablespoon vanilla extract
Pinch of cinnamon
Pinch of salt

Combine the walnuts, dates and 1/3 cup baking cocoa in a food processor and process until chopped to the consistency of coarse crumbs. Press firmly in an 8×8-inch pan.

Combine the avocados, agave nectar, 1/4 cup baking cocoa, the vanilla, cinnamon and salt in a blender or mixing bowl. Process or mix until smooth. Spread over the mixture in the pan. Freeze for 1 hour.

Note: Rebecca tells us that this recipe is easy to make and deceptively wonderful. Not only is it made with "good" fats, but it is also low-glycemic, gluten-free, flourless, and vegan. Since it is a treat of healthy fruit and nuts, you will feel no guilt if you nibble on one on the way to work or serve one to the kids as an after-school snack. You can substitute organic almond butter or peanut butter for the walnuts to create a chocolate-peanut butter cup version. To make it ultra-glycemic, substitute prunes for the dates.

Hello Dollies

Makes 2 dozen

1/2 cup (1 stick) butter, melted
1 cup graham cracker crumbs
1 cup (6 ounces) semisweet
    chocolate chips
1 cup (6 ounces) butterscotch chips
1 cup shredded coconut
1 (14-ounce) can sweetened
    condensed milk
1 cup chopped pecans

Preheat the oven to 350 degrees. Pour the butter into a 9×13-inch baking dish. Layer the graham cracker crumbs, chocolate chips, butterscotch chips and coconut in the prepared dish. Drizzle the sweetened condensed milk over the layers and top with the pecans. Bake for 20 to 25 minutes or until golden brown. Cool in the pan on a wire rack. Cut into squares to serve.

Note: You can double the recipe and bake it for a little longer for a thicker cookie.

Pecan Pie Bars

Makes 2 dozen

8 ounces pecans
1/2 cup (1 stick) butter
1 cup packed brown sugar
1/3 cup honey
2 tablespoons heavy cream
3/4 cup (1 1/2 sticks) butter, cut into
    1/2-inch pieces
2 cups all-purpose flour
1/2 cup packed brown sugar
1/2 teaspoon salt

Chop the pecans coarsely in a food processor. Melt 1/2 cup butter in a heavy saucepan and stir in 1 cup brown sugar, the honey and cream. Simmer for 1 minute, stirring constantly. Stir in the pecans. Keep warm.

Preheat the oven to 350 degrees. Combine 3/4 cup butter, the flour, 1/2 cup brown sugar and the salt in a food processor and process until the mixture forms small crumbs. Sprinkle in a greased 9×13-inch baking pan. Press the mixture down evenly with a metal spatula. Bake on the center oven rack for 20 minutes or until golden brown.

Spread the pecan topping over the hot shortbread. Bake for 20 minutes longer or until the topping is bubbly. Cool in the pan on a wire rack. Cut into twenty-four bars. Store, covered, at room temperature for up to 5 days.

Raspberry Oatmeal Bars

Makes 16 bars

1 1/4 cups quick-cooking oats
1 1/4 cups all-purpose flour
1/2 cup packed brown sugar
1 teaspoon baking powder
1/4 teaspoon salt
14 tablespoons unsalted butter, melted
1 cup raspberry jam or raspberry
    preserves
3/4 cup white chocolate chips
1/4 cup chopped almonds

Preheat the oven to 350 degrees. Mix the oats, flour, brown sugar, baking powder and salt in a large bowl. Add the butter and stir to moisten well. Reserve 1 cup of the oats mixture. Press the remaining oats mixture over the bottom of an 8×8-inch baking pan. Bake for 10 minutes.

Spread the raspberry jam to within 1/4 inch of the edges of the baked layer. Sprinkle with 1/2 cup of the white chocolate chips. Combine the remaining 1/4 cup white chocolate chips with the reserved oats mixture and the almonds in a bowl. Sprinkle over the layers, pressing down lightly to the edges of the pan.

Bake for 25 to 30 minutes longer or until golden brown. Cool completely on a wire rack. Cut into bars to serve.

Candied Orange Peels

Serves 16 or more

8 medium to large oranges
1¹/₂ cups sugar
³/₄ cup water
1 cup sugar

Cut the oranges into quarters. Remove the sections from the peel with a large spoon, leaving about ¹/₈-inch peels. Reserve the orange sections for another use. Cut the peels into ¹/₄-inch strips.

Combine the orange peels with enough water to cover in a saucepan. Bring to a boil. Drain and repeat the process two times to soften the peels.

Combine 1¹/₂ cups sugar with ³/₄ cup water in a saucepan. Add the orange peels and bring to a simmer. Simmer for 20 to 45 minutes or until the syrup forms a thread when poured from the spoon, 230 to 234 degrees on a candy thermometer.

Drain in a large mesh sieve. Spread the peels in a single layer on waxed paper on a tray. Let stand for 8 hours or until completely dry. Toss with 1 cup sugar and store in airtight containers.

Lisi Harrison's Chocolate Spiders

Serves 12

2 cups (12 ounces) butterscotch chips
2 cups (12 ounces) semisweet
    chocolate chips
2½ cups crispy Chinese noodles
1⅔ cups Spanish peanuts

Combine the butterscotch chips and chocolate chips in a double boiler. Cook over simmering water until melted, stirring to blend well. Stir in the noodles and peanuts. Drop by spoonfuls onto waxed paper. Let stand for 1 hour or until firm.

While living in New York City, Lisi Harrison created and developed shows for MTV such as One Bad Trip *and* Room Raiders. *Her time at MTV inspired her to write* The Clique, Best Friends for Never, *and twelve additional books for the series. These best-selling novels for 'tweens and teens have sold millions of copies, and* The Clique *movie was released in 2008. She now resides in Laguna Beach and writes full time beachside. Lisi challenges you to eat just one Chocolate Spider and to let her know if you can—because she can't.*

RECIPE CONTRIBUTORS

*T*he Junior League of Orange County, California, Inc., extends our heartfelt appreciation to the membership, their families, and friends. This wonderful group of supporters contributed more than 400 recipes to make this book possible. To the many members and friends who tested recipes, our genuine appreciation for your time, money, and talents to ensure that our recipes are fabulous. It is our sincere hope that no one has been inadvertently overlooked.

Victoria Ackerman
Jennifer Adams-Goddard
Amy Ainsworth
Catherine "Dixie" Allen
Ambrosia Restaurant and Bar
Amelia's Restaurant
MeeRan Anderson
Antonello Ristorante
A Restaurant
Liana Augustini
Judi Bakly
Kay Bartlett
Edmunds Biters
Courtney Blackwell
Sarah Bridgwater
Sherryl Brightwell
Megan Brief
Taylor Brown
Kristin Buie
Meredith Cagle
Kathy Calegari
Missy Pace Callero
Karen Carboni
Oma Talley Cast

Jeri Lyn Castillo
Charlie Palmer at Bloomingdale's
    South Coast Plaza
Claes Restaurant
Janet Colclasser
Beverly Coulter
Jennifer Dewberry
Disneyland's Blue Bayou Restaurant
Sarah Dressler
Carla Ellek
Maura Ferrero-Baroni
Five Crowns
Cheryl Forberg
Camille Foster
Danielle Friedman
Linda Gerlt
Laura Giles
The Golden Truffle
Ashley Good
Jenny Graham
Kathryn Grant
Loretta Griffin
Berenice Gurski
Suzanne Guy

Chef Jamie Gwen
Nicole Hager
Karla F. Hammond
Elizabeth Hamrick
Mara Hampton
Lu Ann Hancock
Maralou Harrington
Paula Harris
Lisi Harrison
Judy Herman
Rayna Herman
Pokey Huffman
Joanna James
Sonnie Kasch
Tammy Katsekis
Caroline Kavanaugh
Anne Kepple
Katherine Kelly
Kathleen Kelly
Kathy Kelly
Kathy Kerrigan
Kelly Keyes
Susan King
Stacey Kinney

Kiley Kirkpatrick

Tina Knapp

Jennifer Kranawetter

Torrey Boultinghouse Krebs

Tina Kreditor

Karen Kroeter

K'ya Restaurant

Rebecca Lacko

Jo Ann Larsen

Chef Jeff Lavia, Dinner Mojo

Anna Lembke

Maureen Lockwood

Christina Lucey

Susie Luer

Elaine Marshall

Jennifer Martin

Tara Mathiesen

Megan Matt

Lisa McKenzie

Stephanie McNear

Megan Meihaus

Susie Michalski

Diane Mondini

Margaret Morgan

Sue Murphy

Yara Navarre

Celeste Neuhoff

Keely Ng

Christina Nickel

Richard Nixon Library &
    Birthplace Foundation

Brooke North

Kelli Nye

Opah Restaurant and Bar

Anastasia Orbacz

Isabelle Ord

Palm Terrace at the Island Hotel

Laurie Palombo

Kathryn Patton

Louise V. Petersen

Jill Pfeiffer

Tracey Pollack

Aimee Porter

Carla Poulin

Nancy Power

Susan Puskarich

Kate Rader

The Ramos House Café

Faith Records

Katy Reed

Annette Reeves

Barbara Regan

Lisa Rhoads

Kim Riker

Tristan Ritter

Nancy Ringman

Nicole Rogers

Ruby's Diner

Catherine Rudat

Mark Sabre

Jodi Salerno

Heather Saito

Kristin Scheithauer

Julie Schulman

Denise Scott

Donna Sears

Georgia Sewell

Carrie Shapiro

Shanna Siegel

Raymond Skibba

K. C. Stack

Elizabeth Stahr

John Stamos

Ellen Starratt

Dixie Stiegler

Jason Stiegler

Michelle Stiegler

Lauren Steinmann

Cheryl Stockwell

Erin Stone

Tarah Stovall

Dana Strader

Molly Taylor

Cathy Thomas

Dr. Sandra Thompson

Barbara Tone

Kathy Ursini

Erin Varnado

Lori Wagner

The John Wayne Family

Gracey Weisbrod

Diana von Welanetz Wentworth

Vanna White

Amy Yovan

Carol Zalta

Zov's Bistro

RECIPE TESTERS

Marcia Adler

Nicole Anderson

Peter Anderson

Alyssa Artunian

Stephanie Artunian

Liana Augustini

Michelle Baker

Terri Beans

Marisa Bellisimo-Unvert

Denise Berger

Carissa Beyer

Courtney Blackwell

Anne Marie Bohrk

Chara Braman

Megan Brief

Kala Brightwell

Sherryl Brightwell

Kimberly Bucher

Kristin Buie

Meredith Cagle

Carrie Campbell

Oma Tally Cast

Jennifer Castillo

Connie Clem

Shauna Clustka-Good

Sarah Cohen

Kelly Cornell

Bev Coulter

Carla Craft

Sophie Cripe

Cindy Das

Carla Dillon

Kim Domer

Sarah Dressler

Linda Elftmann

Heidi Endert

Susana Ertac

Coco Fabre

Cammie Flatley

Camille Foster

Noelle Gamber

Deanna Garcia

Lawana Gibbs

Jennifer Gonzales

Amy Grady

Suzanne Guy

Nicole Hager

Mara Hampton

Beth Hamrick

Paula Harris

Tammy Harter

Karyn Hartford

Cherie Hemphill

Jennifer Henderson

Rayna Herman

Laura Horn

Marisa Ippolito

Joanna James

Amy Kelly

Kathy Kelly

Kelly Keyes

Stacey Kinney

Christine Knoke

Robyn Korengold

Jennifer Kranawetter

Ben Kroeter

Janice Kroeter

Karen Kroeter

Diane Lawson

Susie Luer

Christina Markl

Elaine Marshall

Jane Martin

Jennifer Martin

Debbie Masek

Tara Mathiesen

Dana McCollum

Roberta McCollom

Melissa McGee

Laura McNair

Betty Middleton

K. J. Mitchell

Jane Mooney

Amber Moyle

Laurel Murray

Keely Ng

Stacy Nichols

Anastasia Orbacz

Nicole Paproski

Yuki Pitkin

Carla Poulin

Erin Pysnik

Cheri Quigley

Kate Rader

Beth Rautiola

Katy Reed

Kim Reynolds

Jennifer Risner

Tristan Ritter

Julie Robbins

Claudine Roberts

Peggy Rodriguez

Angie Rowe

Heather Saito

Kimberly Santamaria

Marisa Schaeffer

Kristin Scheithauer

Cindy Schmude

Rosia Sehn

Letia Short

Shanna Siegel

Nicole Smith

Cynthia Stewart

Jason Stiegler

Michelle Stiegler

Nedka Stills

Lauren Stock

Erin Stone

Dana Strader

Ann Sullivan

Nicole Tardi

Molly Taylor

Dr. Sandra Thompson

Lindsay Ayres Todd

Stephanie Traeger

Lydia Tyler

Kathy Ursini

Albert Valdez

Erin Varnado

Kim Vershave

Kim Vogel

Jessica Vollebregt

Tanya von Mittenwald

Lori Wagner

LaShawn Ware

Gracey Weisbrod

Keri Welhart

Sue Wicks

Camron Wilson

Amy Yovan

Recipe Index

For additional copies of

Orange
County *Fare* a culinary journey through the
California Riviera

please visit our Web site, www.jlocc.org,
or telephone The Junior League of Orange County, California, Inc.,
cookbook office at 949-263-3783